A TWILIGHT STRUGGLE

The Life of John Fitzgerald Kennedy

Barbara Harrison
and
Daniel Terris

Lothrop, Lee & Shepard Books   New York

Copyright © 1992 by Barbara Harrison and Daniel Terris

All rights reserved. No part of this book may be reproduced or utilized in any form or by any means, electronic or mechanical, including photocopying and recording, or by any information storage and retrieval system, without permission in writing from the Publisher. Inquiries should be addressed to Lothrop, Lee & Shepard Books, a division of William Morrow & Company, Inc., 1350 Avenue of the Americas, New York, New York 10019. Printed in the United States of America.

First Edition 1 2 3 4 5 6 7 8 9 10

Library of Congress Cataloging in Publication Data

Harrison, Barbara. A twilight struggle : the life of John Fitzgerald Kennedy / by Barbara Harrison and Daniel Terris. p. cm. Includes bibliographical references. Summary: Discusses the childhood, family, and political career of the president who served from 1961 until his assassination in 1963. ISBN 0-688-08830-9 1. Kennedy, John F. (John Fitzgerald), 1917–1963—Juvenile literature. 2. Presidents—United States—Biography—Juvenile literature. [1. Kennedy, John F. (John Fitzgerald), 1917–1963. 2. Presidents.] I. Terris, Daniel. II. Title. E842.Z9H27 1992 973.922'092—dc20 [B] 91-14926 CIP AC

The photographs in this book are primarily from the archives of the John Fitzgerald Kennedy Library and are reprinted with its permission and courtesy. The photo of the Kennedy family on the title page is reproduced with permission of Bachrach Studios; the photo of the funeral on page 124 is reproduced with permission of UPI/Bettman Newsphotos; the photos of Lyndon Johnson on page 63 and Martin Luther King, Jr., on page 66 are reprinted courtesy of the Boston University photo archives.

A Twilight Struggle

For Benjamin, Eli,
Theodore, Nicholas, Elena,
and Stephen
"One could do worse than be a swinger of birches."

"Now the trumpet summons us again—not as a call to arms, though arms we need—not as a call to battle, though embattled we are—but as a call to bear the burden of a long twilight struggle, year in and year out, 'rejoicing in hope, patient in tribulation,'—a struggle against the common enemies of man: tyranny, poverty, disease and war itself."

—John F. Kennedy
Inaugural Address
January 20, 1961

Contents

Birches

When I see birches bend to left and right
Across the lines of straighter darker trees,
I like to think some boy's been swinging them.
But swinging doesn't bend them down to stay
As ice-storms do. Often you must have seen them
Loaded with ice a sunny winter morning
After a rain. They click upon themselves
As the breeze rises, and turn many-colored
As the stir cracks and crazes their enamel.
Soon the sun's warmth makes them shed crystal shells
Shattering and avalanching on the snow-crust—
Such heaps of broken glass to sweep away
You'd think the inner dome of heaven had fallen.
They are dragged to the withered bracken by the load,
And they seem not to break; though once they are bowed
So low for long, they never right themselves:
You may see their trunks arching in the woods
Years afterwards, trailing their leaves on the ground
Like girls on hands and knees that throw their hair
Before them over their heads to dry in the sun.
But I was going to say when Truth broke in
With all her matter-of-fact about the ice-storm
I should prefer to have some boy bend them
As he went out and in to fetch the cows—
Some boy too far from town to learn baseball,
Whose only play was what he found himself,
Summer or winter, and could play alone.
One by one he subdued his father's trees
By riding them down over and over again
Until he took the stiffness out of them,

And not one but hung limp, not one was left
For him to conquer. He learned all there was
To learn about not launching out too soon
And so not carrying the tree away
Clear to the ground. He always kept his poise
To the top branches, climbing carefully
With the same pains you use to fill a cup
Up to the brim, and even above the brim.
Then he flung outward, feet first, with a swish,
Kicking his way down through the air to the ground.
So was I once myself a swinger of birches.
And so I dream of going back to be.
It's when I'm weary of considerations,
And life is too much like a pathless wood
Where your face burns and tickles with the cobwebs
Broken across it, and one eye is weeping
From a twig's having lashed across it open.
I'd like to get away from earth awhile
And then come back to it and begin over.
May no fate willfully misunderstand me
And half grant what I wish and snatch me away
Not to return. Earth's the right place for love:
I don't know where it's likely to go better.
I'd like to go by climbing a birch tree,
And climb black branches up a snow-white trunk
Toward heaven, till the tree could bear no more,
But dipped its top and set me down again.
That would be good both going and coming back.
One could do worse than be a swinger of birches.

Robert Frost

A Twilight Struggle

1

"The President Is Dead"
(November 22, 1963)

**Such heaps of broken glass to sweep away
You'd think the inner dome of heaven had fallen.**

At 11:40 A.M. the president's plane landed at Love Field in Dallas, Texas. Within ten minutes President and Mrs. John F. Kennedy were in a motorcade on their way to the Trade Mart, where the president was scheduled to speak. The early morning rain had stopped, and Secret Service agents removed the plastic top from the presidential limousine. In the jump seats in front of the Kennedys sat Governor and Mrs. John B. Connally.

President Kennedy was tall, broad-shouldered, and athletic—certainly a far cry from the skinny, narrow-faced kid called "Rat-face" by his Choate School classmates. His eyes were gray-green and had the ability to single out a person in a crowd to create a special bond. Despite almost constant back pain, his stride was graceful.

"I feel great," the president had commented before he left Washington, D.C. "My back feels better than it's felt in years." At the summit of his career, Kennedy was a man in perfect control, at the height of his powers, seemingly favored by the gods. He loved his job and was delighted that Jacqueline, his wife, who rarely accompanied him on political trips, had agreed to join him on this one.

President and Mrs. Kennedy arrive in Dallas on November 22, 1963.

Several people had advised President Kennedy not to go to Texas, a state known as a center of violent extremist political activity. "Dallas is a very dangerous place," Senator J. William Fulbright of Arkansas had warned. "I wouldn't go there. Don't *you* go." Congressman Hale Boggs of Louisiana had told the president that he was about to enter "a hornet's nest." But crowds in San Antonio, Houston, and Fort Worth, where the president had stopped on Thursday, had been friendly and enthusiastic. As he waved at the smiling faces of the thousands of people lining the Dallas parade route, he felt confident that he could win votes for the Democratic party.

In the morning, before boarding the plane, Kennedy had talked to his wife and his special assistant, Kenneth O'Donnell, about the risk of assassination.

"If somebody wants to shoot me from a window with a rifle, nobody can stop it, so why worry about it?" He had expressed little fear, but he knew that the possibility of violent death was real. Since his election three years before, his life had been threatened thirty-three times. Other presidents had been assassinated—Abraham Lincoln, James Garfield, and William McKinley—and attempts had been made on the lives of Theodore Roosevelt, Franklin Delano Roosevelt, and Harry S Truman.

He talked matter-of-factly about death, but he was not indifferent to it. Not long before, his five-year-old daughter, Caroline, had walked into his White House office carrying the still-warm body of her dead bird. She wanted him to see it before she buried it. He was visibly agitated by the sight and insisted that she take it away. He didn't want to hear about the little grave she was arranging or anything about the funeral service. Rarely had the child seen her father so upset. The lifeless bird reminded the president of other deaths—personal losses that Caroline was still too young to understand.

As the limousine moved along the forty-five-minute parade route, a taut, wiry man waited, rifle in hand. He stood at a window on the sixth floor of the Texas School Book Depository Building, partly hidden by boxes of books piled at the window. While he waited for the motorcade, he nibbled some fried chicken. A small greasy bag containing the remnants of his lunch lay on the floor next to him. Lee Harvey Oswald was a bitter and distressed loner estranged from his wife and two children. Early that morning he had arrived at his job at the Book Depository Building with a package wrapped in brown paper. He had explained to a coworker that it contained curtain rods in need of repair.

As the president's car approached its destination, Mrs. Connally, pleased at the warm reception the president was getting, turned to him and said, "You sure can't say Dallas doesn't love you, Mr. President." Kennedy waved confidently to the enthusiastic crowd, calling, "Thank you. Thank you."

At 12:30 P.M. on a day that had become uncomfortably warm and humid, a shot rang out. Clutching his throat, the president called out, "My God, I

— 3 —

am hit!'' and slumped toward his wife. The bullet hit Kennedy in the back of the neck, lacerating his right lung and tearing his windpipe as it exited at his throat. Continuing its path, the bullet entered Governor Connally's back.*

The wiry man on the sixth floor was not distracted by the pigeons that scattered at the crack of his rifle. Oswald focused through the telescopic sight, his eyes still on his target some eighty yards away.

Within seconds another shot shattered the president's skull. The impact racked his body, lifted him, then dropped him into the seat "as if he were a rag doll." Bone, brain, and hair splattered through the air.

People on the parade route and in the cavalcade were stunned, confused. Some dropped to the ground for safety. A man grabbed his little daughter in panic and ran. A policeman rammed his motorcycle over a curb and barreled up an embankment with pistol drawn. An amateur photographer captured the event with his home movie camera.

Mrs. Kennedy, inches away from the bullets herself, held the president in her arms. Her clothing was drenched with his blood. She screamed, "Oh, my God, they have shot my husband." In shock she scrambled recklessly onto the back deck of the moving limousine. Clinton J. Hill, a Secret Service agent, leaped onto the bumper and pushed her back into the car. "My God, what are they doing?" she cried. "My God, they've killed Jack, they've killed my husband!"

During the six-minute race to the hospital, Jackie sobbed quietly, repeating again and again, "He's dead—they've killed him—oh, Jack, oh, Jack. I love you." At 12:36 P.M., six minutes after the first shot, the limousine reached the emergency entrance of Parkland Hospital. Governor Connally was lifted onto a stretcher and taken into Trauma Room 2. Jackie cradled her husband in her arms. When Agent Hill said to her, "Please, we must get the president

*This is the official account as given in the Warren Commission Report. Many alternative scenarios have been proposed.

to a doctor," she moaned, "No, Mr. Hill. You know he's dead. Let me alone."

Hill realized that Mrs. Kennedy was hiding her husband from the curious eyes of the crowd, to provide him with what she knew he would want: privacy, dignity, refuge. The agent took off his jacket and gave it to her. She wrapped it gently around the president's head. Only then would she allow him to be lifted to the stretcher. He was wheeled into Trauma Room 1, where doctors frantically tried to revive him.

Mrs. Kennedy demanded to be with her husband during this crisis, and she was admitted to the emergency room. A priest from a nearby church administered last rites. Jackie removed her wedding band and placed it on her husband's finger, comforted by the knowledge that some part of her would be with him forever. She knelt in a pool of his blood and prayed.

Doctors and attendants observed that the EKG needle monitoring the president's heartbeat was still. At 1:00 P.M. one of the doctors looked at Mrs. Kennedy and said, "Your husband has sustained a fatal wound." Not sure she had understood, a second physician said, "The president is gone." Trying to master his own emotion, he repeated, "The president is dead."

Jackie made no gasp, no groan. She had known that from the first.

John Fitzgerald Kennedy. (1918)

2

Young Jack
(1917–1946)

**He learned all there was
To learn about not launching out too soon.**

"She had the doctors crazy, she had her babies so fast," one friend commented.

Even Rose Fitzgerald Kennedy was amazed. "I don't drink, I don't smoke, but I have lots of children." In all, she would bear nine.

Rose was a stickler for organization. She scrupulously kept an index file of information about her children, ranging from medical examinations to shoe sizes. When her second child was born, Rose made the following entry:

John Fitzgerald Kennedy
born Brookline, Mass. (83 Beals Street) May 29, 1917

At three o'clock on that uncommonly cold and cloudy Tuesday afternoon, Dr. Frederick Good and two attendants helped Rose Kennedy in the birth. They were in the master bedroom of the Kennedys' green clapboard house in Brookline, a town just west of Boston.

Rose Elizabeth (Fitzgerald) Kennedy was twenty-six years old, and her

Joseph P. Kennedy at his graduation from Harvard. (1912) He became a millionaire by the age of 35.

Rose Fitzgerald as a young woman (c. 1911). Jack called his mother "the glue that held the family together."

husband, Joseph Patrick Kennedy, was twenty-eight. The tiny blue-eyed baby was named in honor of Rose's father, John Francis Fitzgerald, the popular Boston politician known as Honey Fitz. The boy would soon be called Jack. His older brother, Joe, Jr., had been born two years earlier.

The second entry on Jack's index card noted normal childhood diseases: "whooping cough, measles, chicken pox." The third listed "scarlet fever— February 20, 1920." Scarlet fever was a highly contagious, life-threatening disease, particularly for young children. Rose and Joseph Kennedy were frantic that their other children would be infected—Joseph, Jr., as well as Rosemary, born the year after Jack's birth, and Kathleen, born just as he became sick. They were terrified about Jack's chances of survival.

Jack's father had never been so close to serious illness. Every day he spent hours in the hospital by his son's side, watching his face flush with fever. He found it difficult to wrench himself away from the sterile hospital room where his second child was struggling for breath. He vowed to God that if the boy was spared, he would give half of his savings to charity.

About the third week in March, as winter gave way to spring, Jack at last took a turn for the better. He spent four more weeks in the hospital and then two weeks at a health spa in Poland Springs, Maine. His illness was long and painful and caused a rude separation from his family—an ordeal that lasted for three months.

When Jack recovered, his father gratefully presented a check in the amount of $3,700 to the Guild of St. Appolonia. Although it is unlikely that Joe Kennedy, whose fortunes were rapidly increasing, was worth less than $7,500, he felt that he had fulfilled his bargain with God.

Jack learned at an early age to scramble for attention in the frenzy of the Kennedy household. By 1925 the family included Eunice, Patricia, and Robert. The Kennedys had moved in 1920 from Beals Street to a house a few blocks away, on the corner of Naples and Abbotsford roads, a sprawling place with twelve rooms, turreted windows, and a porch halfway around it. Jack's father was busy becoming a successful banker and movie tycoon, and spent long periods away from home. His mother was active with the demands of raising seven children, directing a growing household staff, and keeping up with her social, civic, and religious obligations.

With her sparrow's build and indomitable will, Rose Kennedy was the driving force in the Kennedy household. Disciplined herself, she sought to teach discipline. Lunch was served at one-fifteen—not a minute sooner or a minute later—and dinner promptly at seven. There were clocks in every room so no one would be late. She kept track of her children at the beach by equipping them with different-colored bathing caps. Orderly conduct at home and at school won Rose's greatest favor, and she was not shy about using the paddle to enforce her rules.

Try as he might, Jack never came to terms with his mother's system. He enviously watched his older brother shine in her eyes. Joe, Jr., was an extension of his father, a robust, extroverted go-getter. His parents praised him as a model child. When he was a boy, he declared his intention to become the first Roman Catholic president of the United States. No one, including Jack, doubted for a moment that he would be. Rose and Joe, Sr., could not disguise their affection for their favored first son. Joe, Jr., would always be a little taller, a little faster, a little better-behaved. How could the younger boy compete?

So Jack took a different direction. He left his clothes piled in a mound on the bedroom floor. He rarely tucked in his shirt. Money seemed to slip through his pockets. He let his attention wander in school. He ignored the clocks and straggled in late for meals. "Most of the children were reasonably prompt," Rose said, "but Jack was at the bottom of the class."

But he made his mother laugh. Rose, like her husband, had been brought up a strict Roman Catholic, and she wanted religion to be as important to her children as it was to her. One Good Friday, Rose called her children together for prayer. Since the day commemorated Christ's Crucifixion, Rose asked each of her children to pray for a happy death. While Joe, Jr., and the others bowed their heads reverently, freckle-faced Jack, with ears much too large for his head, looked up and announced that what *he* prayed for was two dogs. His mother had to work hard to conceal her amusement.

At home or away, Jack's father made a powerful impression. The children were wide-eyed when he returned home in a sleek Rolls-Royce. From Hollywood he brought back the best movies of the day for the children and their friends to view in the family projection room. His glamorous life brought him in touch with baseball giant Babe Ruth, popular cowboy star Tom Mix, and Jack's personal hero, Red Grange, a spectacular football player. The children were thrilled about the possibility of meeting these people.

As a young Irish Catholic boy making his way through Protestant, upper-crust Harvard College, Joe had sworn that he would make a million dollars by the time he was thirty-five. It had taken bending the rules a bit—a polit-

Joe, Jr., and Jack at their family's summer home in Hyannis Port, Massachusetts. (c. 1925)

At the Dexter School in Brookline, Massachusetts, Jack and Joe, Jr., played on the football team. In this 1926 photograph, Jack is nine years old and in the fourth grade. He is seated on the ground, at the right. Joe, Jr., is third from the left, second row from the front.

ical favor here, a tip from a friend there—but Joe Kennedy had reached his goal, and he demanded similar achievements from his children.

Joe wanted for his sons no less than he wanted for himself: fame, power, high political office. His words became a family rallying cry: "We want no losers around here, only winners." These excessively high expectations placed a heavy burden on both Jack and Joe, Jr. For both, losing was more than humiliation. It was a fate worse than death.

Everything in the Kennedy household was a fierce competition. Report cards were a matter of family discussion. The brothers and sisters raced against one

The Kennedy children at Hyannis Port. (1928)

another on sailboats at the family's summer home in Hyannis Port, Massachusetts. At the breakfast table, Rose and Joe gave quizzes on current events. Small talk was discouraged. "Nothing trivial was ever discussed at the table" if Rose could help it.

Jack had to be steadfast on the baseball field, where Joe, Jr., pitched and Jack was catcher. Sometimes Joe, Jr., threw the ball so hard that he knocked his brother down. Jack was often in tears, and to his brother's disgust, he frequently dropped the ball. Although Joe, Jr., was patient with his other brothers and sisters, he was often a hot-tempered bully with Jack.

On one occasion, Joe, Jr., suggested a bicycle race. He proposed that the boys start in front of the house and ride around the block in opposite directions. Jack hopped onto his bike and pedaled furiously, hoping that for once he could beat his older brother at his own game. At the final corner, he saw Joe coming toward him from the other end of the block. The sidewalk was narrow, and Jack could see that if they both dashed for the finish line, there would be trouble. Maybe Joe, Jr., expected that his little brother would back down, accept defeat. But Jack smelled victory and pressed ahead. Neither boy gave way to the other, and they collided head-on by the front steps of the house. Joe, Jr., walked away unscathed. Jack needed twenty-eight stitches.

Even if he hadn't been two years younger, Jack would have had a hard time keeping up. Although he "could fight like fury when he had to," he was slighter in build than Joe, Jr., and more vulnerable. Throughout his childhood, his bedroom served as a fortress, where he spent his time alone while he recuperated from persistent ailments—bronchitis, diphtheria, stomach trouble, flu, colds, and allergies. "When we were growing up together, we used to laugh about the great risk a mosquito took in biting Jack Kennedy—with some of his blood the mosquito was almost sure to die," his brother Bobby said later.

Of course, Jack discovered that being sick had its advantages too. People fussed and fretted over him. Even at two, he charmed the nurses who helped him recover from scarlet fever. They practically lined up to visit him in Brookline after he left the hospital. Later on, being sick—or, at times, perhaps feigning illness—gained his mother's attention and gave him an excuse for not living up to the standards set by his older brother.

Books became Jack's constant companions. They prodded his imagination and helped him to see through the eyes of others. They also provided an escape from family pressures. As a young boy, he loved animal adventure stories. As he grew older, the legends of King Arthur appealed to his growing inclination toward idealism. He returned to the tales of King Arthur and the Round Table so often that the book became dog-eared and tattered. Later, history and biography absorbed him. He had almost photographic recall. Whole passages, scenes, and characters lived in his mind.

Jack developed a playful relationship with his younger brothers and sisters. Whereas Joe, Jr., assumed the role of a small adult, the commander in chief of the Kennedy kingdom, Jack enchanted them with good-natured wit and humor. His sister Kathleen—called "Kick"—talkative, energetic, and popular, became his closest ally. He protected Rosemary, who was mentally retarded, and he was a Pied Piper, leading the younger siblings in games and stories. But beneath that lightheartedness was a struggle for the affection and admiration of his parents—and his older brother. He developed a stiff upper lip and self-control to disguise his deep emotions and high spirits. When he was older, friends observed something in Jack that seemed lonely and apart.

The boy's temperament did not stop him from plunging into the rough public world of Boston politics. As a young child, he was enraptured when his grandfather John Fitzgerald rehearsed his political speeches. The boy accompanied Honey Fitz to political rallies, walked with him through Boston neighborhoods as he campaigned, and watched him do a soft-shoe dance and burst out with a verse of a sentimental Irish song.

All the Kennedys grew up with the story of Honey Fitz's heroism at a neighborhood baseball game. The former mayor of Boston saved dozens of children by pushing them out of the way of a careening truck. Before he could dodge, the truck ran over his legs and badly injured him. Nonetheless, as he lay on the field, waiting for medical help, he let the crowd know he was all right by singing "Sweet Adeline."

Jack also learned something about politics from his grandfather Kennedy. Patrick Joseph Kennedy was a saloon keeper and political boss in East Boston. He sported a prominent handlebar mustache and was called "one of the shrewdest men in Boston politics."

Jack Kennedy's great-grandparents had come to the United States on the immigrant "coffin ships" of the 1840s, where incredible numbers of people died en route. They had been forced out of Ireland by the great famine caused by the failure of their main food source, potatoes. From their rough-hewn, thatch-roofed cottages in County Wexford, the Fitzgeralds and the Kennedys had made the journey to the New World, where they had inched their way to better lives despite appalling living conditions and brutal anti-Irish prejudice.

By the 1920s, Catholic Irish Americans were firmly in control of the political life of Boston, but old-time Protestant Yankees still controlled most of the money and the banks and universities that dominated New England life. Despite his increasing fortune, Joe Kennedy knew that he would always be an outsider in Boston. When a Boston newspaper repeatedly called him an Irishman, Joe flew into a rage: "Goddam it! I was born in this country. My children were born in this country. What the hell does someone have to do to become an American?"

In 1927, when Jack was ten years old, Joe Kennedy moved his family from Massachusetts to the Riverdale section of The Bronx, New York. There the Kennedys could be free of Boston anti-Irish prejudice and Joe would be closer to his financial dealings. Another child, Jean, was born in 1928.

The growing family spent summers at their home in Hyannis Port, Massachusetts. Jack and Joe, Jr., sailed the tricky waters of Nantucket Sound on their twenty-five-foot sloop, *Victura*—victory. Joe, Sr., beamed when his two oldest sons rescued a sailor stranded in high seas whom they spotted from their porch. Grandpa Honey Fitz called the story in to the Boston *Post*, and the paper carried an article about the daring exploit of the two boys, aged twelve and ten.

The stock market crashed in 1929, and the United States plunged into the Great Depression. But while ruined Wall Street stockbrokers jumped out of skyscrapers to their deaths and millions of Americans lost their jobs, Joe Kennedy managed to keep his fortune intact. As members of a rich and privileged family, the Kennedy children had tutors for schoolwork, skippers for sailing, coaches for swimming, and teachers for piano and dancing. Every morning in Hyannis Port, as the sun came up, Jack was on the lawn with Joe, Jr., doing calisthenics under the direction of a physical education instructor who, legend has it, could be heard from Nantucket Sound to Cape Cod Bay.

As Jack and Joe, Jr., grew older, their rivalry intensified. They engaged in brutal fights that left their brothers and sisters cowering. Bobby, eight years younger than Jack, stood in tears with his hands over his ears as he witnessed the battles.

When he was fourteen, in 1931, Jack followed Joe, Jr., to the Choate School, a renowned preparatory school in Wallingford, Connecticut. During Jack's first year at Choate, his youngest brother, Edward (Teddy), was born. Even away from his family, Jack continued to live in the shadow of his older brother. Joe, Jr., was on varsity teams in several sports, but Jack was plagued by allergies, asthma, flu, and a mysterious illness that left him limp and exhausted. He was so sick that he missed the spring term of his third year at Choate.

A family friend remembers visiting Jack in a hospital room at about this time. Jack was lying in bed reading *The World Crisis* by Winston Churchill, so submerged by books that his pale face was barely visible. He continued to be fascinated by history and was the only boy at the school to subscribe to the *New York Times*. He showed a flair for writing and great skill at the popular radio quiz game *Information, Please*. But he frustrated his housemaster, who complained to the school head that "Jack studies at the last minute, keeps appointments late, has little sense of material value, and can seldom locate his possessions." Disgusted by Jack's messy room, the housemaster made surprise inspections, and he occasionally dumped all of Jack's belongings in a big pile on the floor to force him to clean house.

Jack was a leader of the Muckers Club, a rowdy group of Choate boys who constantly played pranks on the school authorities. Once, when Rose Kennedy sent her son a crate of oranges from Florida, he entertained himself by throwing them, one by one, out the window at his friends. Another time he purposely woke the housemaster at 6:00 A.M. by loudly bouncing his trunk down the steps on the way to storing it in the cellar.

It was to Lem Billings, his roommate and best friend, that Jack confided the mixed emotions that he felt about his brother. Rose, Joe, Sr., and Grandpa and Grandma Fitzgerald were at Choate the day that Joe, Jr., was awarded the coveted Harvard Trophy, given to the student who best combined scholarship and sportsmanship. Although Jack was pleased by his brother's triumph, he was also envious when he saw the glowing pride on his father's face.

That day Jack and Lem took a long walk away from the cheering crowd. Each shared feelings of hurt in a heart-to-heart talk. For the first time, Jack told Lem that he believed that he was smarter than Joe, Jr., but that his mind worked in a different way. When Jack graduated from Choate two years later, he was just sixty-fourth in a class of one hundred sixteen. Nevertheless, he was voted "most likely to succeed" by his classmates, demonstrating his popularity and growing political savvy. He and his buddies campaigned for various accolades—"wittiest," "handsomest," "most likely to succeed"—and they traded votes to win.

Jack tried to break the family mold by enrolling at Princeton instead of

Members of the Muckers Club at the Choate School. Left to right: Ralph Horton, Lem Billings, Butch Schriber, and Jack Kennedy. (c. 1934)

Much to his mother's chagrin, Jack wore old, scuffed saddle shoes on the day of his graduation from Choate in 1935.

Harvard. After a serious attack of hepatitis, he withdrew in the fall of his freshman year. Rather than return to Princeton, he bowed to family pressure and followed his father's and brother's footsteps, enrolling at Harvard in the fall of 1936.

Times had changed since Jack's father had felt the sting of anti-Irish prejudice as a Harvard student. Jack Kennedy was young and wealthy and was elected to such snobbish Harvard groups as the Hasty Pudding Club, a drama society, and the Spee, a social club. He lived in the Harvard house named for John Winthrop, the first governor of Massachusetts.

Despite being what his coach called "a big tall stringbean," the 145-pound,

Jack practicing at the Harvard University swimming pool. Although he was a good athlete, he never lived up to his own high expectations. (*Boston Globe*, c. 1937–1938.)

6-foot freshman was determined to succeed in college athletics. He was never heavy enough to play varsity football. During a junior varsity practice game against the varsity squad, he was tackled hard and suffered a badly ruptured spinal disk, which caused a back injury that would torment him for the rest of his life. Thereafter, he confined his athletic efforts to the swim team.

A testimony to Jack's stamina and perseverance was his secret pact with his Harvard roommate, Torbert Macdonald. Despite a bout of flu that sent him to the infirmary, Jack was determined to win his Harvard letter in swimming. Every day Torb would slip into the infirmary with food for Jack. Then they would leave by the back door for the indoor pool, where Jack rigorously practiced his backstroke. After practice Torb escorted him back to the infirmary. Jack won his varsity letter.

His love of history deepened at Harvard, though his grades remained only average. When his father was appointed ambassador to Great Britain in 1938, Jack turned his attention to England. He adopted as his hero a graceful, stately youth named Raymond Asquith, who was killed in World War I. Asquith, a son of a British prime minister, represented qualities the college student admired: upper-class elegance, grace, the ability to feel deeply about things and yet conceal his emotions. Jack thrived on the trips to London to visit his family and relished the excitement of the world of diplomacy.

On September 1, 1939, however, landmark events shook the world: Germany invaded Poland, marking the start of World War II. Jack, Joe, Jr., and Kick were in the visitor's gallery in the British Parliament two days later when Prime Minister Neville Chamberlain gave his declaration of war against Nazi Germany.

Jack returned to Harvard for his senior year preoccupied by the specter of the war. He wrote his senior thesis about why Great Britain had refused to believe that war with Germany was possible.

On June 20, 1940, Jack Kennedy was graduated, with honors in government, from Harvard. Once again, Jack's mother was disappointed by his sloppy appearance. His father sent him a cablegram from England: TWO THINGS I ALWAYS KNEW ABOUT YOU ONE THAT YOU ARE SMART TWO THAT YOU ARE A SWELL GUY LOVE DAD.

In the fall of 1940, on the eve of the Nazi bombings that terrified Great Britain, Jack's senior thesis was published as the book *Why England Slept*. It became a best-seller in the United States and Great Britain, making the twenty-three-year-old Jack something of a celebrity—and an authority on the war.

Despite his professor's comment that it was "badly written," Jack earned a *magna cum laude* on his college thesis, "Appeasement at Munich," and transformed it into a best-selling book.

He told one radio interviewer that he planned to attend law school. "I'm more or less interested in working sometime in my life for the government," he said, "but I haven't really decided yet."

In the meantime, he was eager to enter the armed services. As ambassador, his father had believed that the United States should keep out of the European conflict. Indeed, Joe, Sr., had a reputation as a Nazi sympathizer. But after Japan's attack on Pearl Harbor on December 7, 1941, the United States declared war on Germany and Japan. Jack tried to enlist in the army but was refused because of his back problem. He started a furious exercise program and begged his father to pull strings so the navy would accept him.

Early in his stint in the navy, Jack had one of the first serious romances of his life. His sister Kick had introduced him to Inga Arvad, a strikingly beautiful Danish journalist whom she had known in Washington, D.C. Jack began dating her but had to keep the relationship a secret from his parents. Not only was Inga not Catholic, which would by itself have concerned Rose Kennedy greatly; she had also been married and divorced twice. An attachment between Jack and such a woman was unthinkable to Rose.

But worse was yet to come. In the winter of 1942 the Washington newspapers discovered a photograph showing Inga sitting next to Adolf Hitler at the 1936 Olympic Games in Germany. Rumors circulated that Inga was or had been a Nazi spy. The FBI investigated. Jack's relationship with Inga became an open secret. He was in danger of discharge from the navy.

At this point Joe Kennedy stepped in. He was more tolerant than Rose about Jack's dating non-Catholics. Joe himself, although devoted to his family, did not live according to the precepts of the Roman Catholic Church. It was widely rumored that he had had many affairs, including a long relationship with movie actress Gloria Swanson. He warned Jack that gossip about Inga's involvement with the Nazis could ruin him. Jack, angry about the rumors, tried to clear her name. Joe arranged to have his son transferred, and the affair with Inga Arvad came to an end.

In March of 1943, Lieutenant (junior grade) Kennedy finally saw action in the war. He was in command of twelve officers and men on a small, speedy patrol boat, PT-109, in the Solomon Islands in the Pacific, the heart of heavy naval action against the Japanese. Two or three times a week, Jack carried on the Kennedy tradition and led before-dinner shipboard discussions about education, politics, and military and world affairs.

PT-109 was split in half by a Japanese destroyer on August 2, 1943. Two of the crew were killed instantly. Jack was slammed hard against the cockpit wall, the steering wheel torn from his grasp. "This is how it feels to be killed," he thought. He just missed being crushed by the steel prow of the destroyer.

Gasoline fires erupted on the water as his crew was buffeted in the fierce wake of the retreating destroyer. He and four crewmen held on to the half of the craft still afloat. Jack called to the others. Six responded.

"Mr. Kennedy! Mr. Kennedy! McMahon is badly hurt," answered Gunner's Mate Charles A. Harris, himself wounded. Jack swam toward Harris's voice. He found machinist Patrick McMahon suffering from hideous burns on his hands and face.

"Go on, skipper. You go on. I've had it," murmured McMahon, who was unable to swim because of his severe wounds. Jack took him in tow and swam hard against a strong current to carry him to the boat. He then went back for Harris, who was ready to give up.

"I can't go any farther," Harris gasped.

"For a guy from Boston, you're certainly putting up a great exhibition out here," Jack snapped back. With his help, Harris made it to the drifting hull.

As dawn approached, it became clear to the crew that the hull was taking on too much water and the boat was sinking. Jack ordered the men to swim to an island about three and a half miles to the southeast. "I'll take Mc-Mahon," he called out to the others. He cut one end of a strap on McMahon's life preserver, clenched it between his teeth, and swam with the machinist on his back, swallowing enormous amounts of water.

Five hours later they drifted to the beach, where Jack collapsed, panting, facedown in the sand. When he tried to stand, he vomited up the seawater, but he and McMahon struggled to the bushes to hide from the enemy.

Jack rallied quickly and was able to watch as the rest of his men touched shore. He then embarked on several expeditions, but returned each time feverish and exhausted. On the sixth day, two islanders discovered the PT-109 campsite, and they carried out a message for help gouged into a coconut shell. The crew of PT-109 was soon saved.

Jack was sent to the United States to recuperate from his injuries. He had aggravated his back problems and contracted a case of malaria that dropped his weight from 150 to 125. Jack went home to convalesce at the Chelsea Naval Hospital in Massachusetts, grateful to be alive. He was proud of himself, as well. He had proved that he could hold his ground in his first real test of leadership. As a war hero, Jack finally received the recognition he hungered for. The story of PT-109 was big news, and the twenty-seven-year-old commander was a sensation. On June 12, 1944, he was awarded the Navy and Marine Corps Medal and a citation for "extremely heroic conduct."

The war years were brutal for the Kennedys. Joe, Sr.'s, early opposition to the war caused him trouble, and he was forced to resign as ambassador to Great Britain. Rosemary, with her mental handicap, became violent. Without telling anyone else in the family, Joe, Sr., allowed her to undergo a dangerous brain operation in 1941 that left her nearly unable to communicate; she was put in an institution. Jack's favorite sister, Kick, married a Protestant English nobleman, and Rose almost broke off ties with her daughter. In August 1944, the most devastating news of all came to the family at the Hyannis Port compound: Joe, Jr., was dead, killed in the skies over England. The following month, Kick's husband was also killed in action.

In the end it was Joe, Jr., who paid the dearest price for the Kennedy family's competitiveness. A navy flier, he had volunteered for an extremely dangerous mission in Europe a month after his full commitment to the navy was complete. There was no obvious reason for his going on that mission. Perhaps, in the wake of Jack's triumph in the South Pacific, Joe, Jr., felt that he would prove or reassert his superiority.

The months after the young pilot's death were bleak for the Kennedy family. For Jack, it was the most difficult time in his life. He had just begun to emerge as an individual, to assert himself in the eyes of his parents and siblings as a war hero, and to show a talent that his older brother had not manifested—writing. Jack lived in the hope of emerging victorious in the rivalry. But with his death Joe, Jr., had closed the door to such a victory. Jack confided to Lem Billings, "I'm shadowboxing a match the shadow is always going to win."

Struggling for a way to express his grief and to comfort his family, Jack once again turned to books. In memory of his brother, he invited family and friends to write memorial essays to be included in a privately published book, *As We Remember Joe*. Although his father could never bear to read more than one section at a time, he was touched by Jack's efforts.

In the essay Jack wrote about Joe, Jr., he spoke about his brother's bravery, but said that Joe had "achieved his greatest success as the older brother." His essay evaded the bitter truth about the competition between the two oldest Kennedy boys. He also hinted at something that perhaps ran deeper than the rivalry: "I do not know anyone with whom I would rather have spent an evening or played golf or, in fact, done anything," wrote the loyal younger brother.

Jack underwent back surgery and recuperated in Phoenix, Arizona. Each day that he was there, his father would call him at precisely 5:00 P.M., and the two would talk about national affairs and politics as if they were sitting at the family dining table. They came together in a way that they never had before.

In spring of 1945, four months before the end of hostilities, Jack spent a month as a reporter at the United Nations founding conference in San Francisco. He wrote sixteen stories for the Hearst newspapers, and he flew to London in June to report on the British elections.

When he returned home, father and son discussed Jack's future. What would the young man do? How would he serve his country? Joe was now convinced that his second son could carry on the family dream of success in politics, but Jack was reluctant.

He was interested in world affairs and problems of government, but he did not see himself as a politician. Outside his immediate family and good friends, he was shy, self-conscious, and more restrained than his brother had been. The thought of campaigning embarrassed him. He saw himself more as a writer, a teacher, a lawyer.

But his father pressed hard. In a tone of exasperation tinged with excitement, Jack commented to his navy buddy Red Fay, "I'm it now, you know. It's my turn. I've got to perform."

Over a year after Joe, Jr.'s, death, Jack decided to run for a vacant seat in Massachusetts's eleventh congressional district. The sprawling eleventh included Boston's North End, where his mother and Honey Fitz had been born, and East Boston, his father's birthplace and his grandfather Kennedy's old home. He rented a modest suite of rooms in the Hotel Bellevue, where his

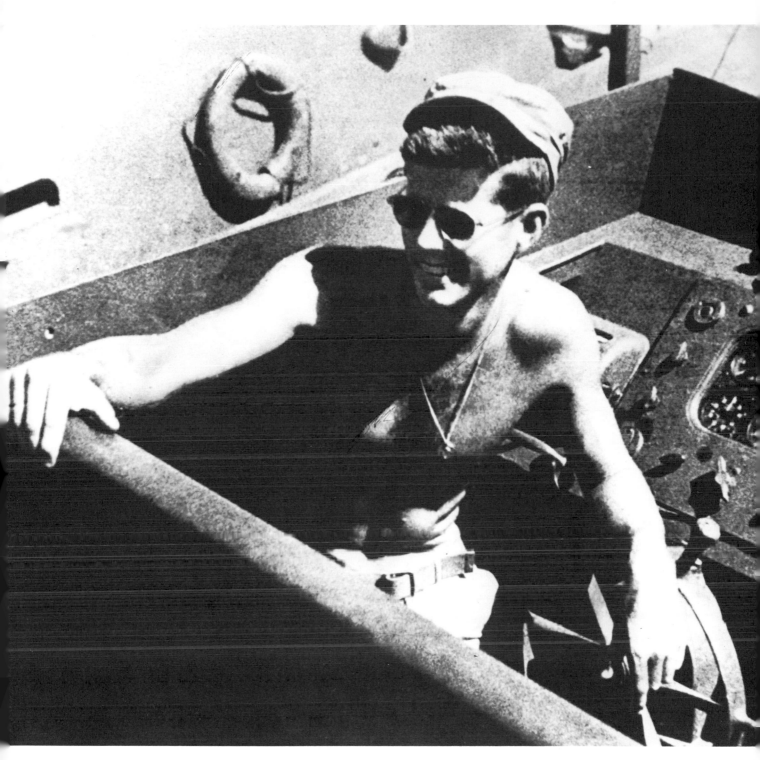

Lt. (jg) John Kennedy at sea. (c. 1943)

(*Left to right*) Jack, Jean, Rose, Joseph, Patricia, Robert, and Eunice. (*Front*)
Edward. (Hyannis Port, c. 1948)

grandfather Honey Fitz lived, and he began seeking people to help him in his bid for political office.

Jack entered politics reluctantly, but once he was in the fray, he was determined to be first. His father's words continued to echo: "We don't want any losers around here."

The young congressman with his father, Joseph, and grandfather John F. "Honey Fitz" Fitzgerald. (1946)

3

The Congressman
(1946–1952)

**He always kept his poise
To the top branches, climbing carefully**

On January 21, 1946, Jack, awkward and ill at ease, climbed three flights of stairs and knocked on the door of a cold-water flat in the Boston neighborhood of Charlestown. A twenty-watt bulb barely lit the hallway. Dave Powers opened the door and, in the dim light, saw a tall, gaunt fellow who held out his hand and said, "My name is Jack Kennedy. I am a candidate for Congress. Will you help me?"

Jack needed supporters like Dave Powers, young men who thrived on local politics. He had to convince the voters of Massachusetts's eleventh congressional district that, at twenty-eight years of age, he was the right man to represent them in Washington.

Jack Kennedy won Dave Powers's friendship. Dave, a war veteran like himself, possessed a keen mind, a sharp wit, and the capacity to love generously. As a boy in Charlestown, he sold newspapers at the Navy Yard to help his struggling family. Before the war Dave had gone from door to door, working on street directories for a publishing house, checking the accuracy of names and addresses. He knew many families and every nook and cranny of Charlestown. He was one of several people who helped Jack in his first political campaign as a paid staff worker—and stayed on for all of them.

Many people considered Jack a carpetbagger, an outsider who returned to Boston to pursue political office. Few Boston politicians thought he could win. But Jack was no stranger to Massachusetts, and his grandfathers on both sides were active in Boston politics. One of the few people who did think he could win was Boston's hard-driving mayor, James Michael Curley, who observed: "With those two names, Fitzgerald and Kennedy, how can he miss?"

But, for Jack Kennedy, victory in the eleventh congressional district was in no way assured. Jack was running in a working-class district and was scoffed at as "a millionaire's son from Harvard." He had attended exclusive schools. He had no political experience. In fact, he had never held a real job. How would the guys who worked long hours in the Navy Yard or on the docks respond to him?

When Patrick J. "Patsy" Mulkern, savvy political veteran, met him for the first time, he clamored, "For the love of Christ, take the sneakers off, Jack. You think you're going to play golf?" Mulkern later recalled, "We had a hell of a job with him."

One thing that set Jack apart from old-style Boston politicians like Mayor Curley and his grandpa Fitzgerald was that he did not wear a hat. He was urged to wear one as a show of support for the state's hat industry and to make him appear older, more mature. But Jack considered his mop of unruly hair a political asset.

Joe Kane, an experienced Irish-American politician, developed a campaign theme to be echoed throughout Jack's political life: "The New Generation Offers a Leader—John F. Kennedy." Kane told Joe Kennedy, "Your Jack is worth a king's ransom."

But Jack wasn't convinced that people would like him. He appeared sickly and hollow-eyed, a tall, thin reed. In front of an audience, Jack was nervous. He tended to stutter and stumble over words. As he spoke, his eyes were glued to the written text. His voice was scratchy, his delivery too serious. Jack

Jack Kennedy on the stump during his first political campaign. (1946)

worried that his speeches were so boring that they put people to sleep. His biggest stumbling block was that he was painfully self-conscious. Apologetically, Jack sometimes explained, "If Joe were alive, I wouldn't be in this. I'm only trying to fill his shoes."

Yet he seemed to be getting through to people. Once, when he stumbled over a word, he flashed a winning smile that lit up the room. He communicated something real, something genuine.

When a troublemaker heckled Jack about his father's money, Jack said, "I don't have to apologize for my father or any of the Kennedys. I'm running for Congress. Let's stick to that. If you want to talk to me about my family, I'll meet you outside." It was one of the few times Jack Kennedy lost his composure.

Despite his sallow complexion and bag-of-bones appearance, the six-foot-one candidate was determined to shake the hand of every voter in the eleventh district. He displayed an amazing capacity for work. "I would get him out of bed at the Bellevue Hotel around six-thirty in the morning," said Dave Powers. Jack, shirttails barely tucked in, rushed to the Charlestown Navy Yard, where he would shake hands with thousands of workers on their way to work. He listened to what they had to say. "It was hard to disengage him and drag him away," observed Powers.

People found something fresh, vigorous, and disarming in Jack. Unkempt in appearance, he looked as if he needed caring for, and he had a way of putting people at ease. He would grab a hamburger and a milk shake, and then stop at the barbershop, the grocery, the candy store, and the fire station before returning to the Navy Yard to catch the workers on their way home.

Campaigning was grueling work. Jack called it a treadmill. And for Jack, it was even tougher than for many people. He was ailing much of the time. His back was bothering him. At times he was brought to tears by exhaustion. He sometimes despaired that he had ever agreed to run for political office. But he rarely complained. He pushed himself harder, always harder. During the campaign he averaged four-and-a-half hours sleep a night.

Just before dinner he would soak in a tub of hot water to ease his constant back pain. He often greeted people from the bathroom with his clipped Boston accent—"I'm in heah"—and carried on serious conversations. A board was stretched across the tub with a razor, a book rest, and a profusion of books. A familiar sight in his apartment was open books with pages drying out after a tumble into the tub.

Jack's family and old friends were at his side. Eunice and Jean, with Jean's roommate Ethel Skakel, worked in the Boston office while twenty-one-year-old Bobby, just out of the navy, knocked on doors in East Cambridge. Their father, deeply interested, worked diligently behind the scenes. Joe Kennedy approved every decision Jack made and attended to every detail of the campaign. He also paid all the campaign expenses.

Paul B. (Red) Fay, Jr., Jack's navy friend, arrived from California to help. Harvard pals of the Kennedy brothers joined the campaign: Torb Macdonald (Jack's roommate), Timothy J. Reardon (Joe, Jr.'s), and Kenny O'Donnell (Bobby's). Although Lem Billings, Jack's Choate School friend, planned to work for only two or three weeks, he stayed through the entire campaign. These people would remain lifelong friends.

A persuasive campaign tactic was the distribution of reprints of John Hersey's article on Jack's heroism in the South Pacific, written for *The New Yorker* and reprinted in *Reader's Digest*. In "Survival," Hersey described the destruction of the PT boat by the Japanese destroyer and Jack's bravery in rising to the occasion. The article had a tremendous impact on voters.

The *Reader's Digest* reprint was a huge success for the Kennedy camp, "a knockout blow," as one campaign worker put it. A story went around that after one of the opposing candidates' wives read the reprint, she said she'd have to vote for Jack.

Rose Kennedy was a great help to Jack in the campaign. She hosted gatherings all over the district, and she talked about the challenge of raising her children. She mentioned the index cards listing important dates in their lives and shared stories about her glamorous life in England. Inevitably she received a standing ovation.

On June 17, 1946, Bunker Hill Day, the day before the primary election that was to mark his baptism in political waters, Jack walked five miles in a holiday parade. He was pushing himself to the limit. Physically and emotionally exhausted, Jack collapsed just past the reviewing stand and recovered at the home of a supporter.

The following day Jack Kennedy won the election, nearly doubling the vote of his nearest competitor. Feeling much better, his eyes brimming with tears, he thanked his campaign workers and dashed off with Grandpa Fitzgerald to see the Marx Brothers in *A Night in Casablanca*. He had won his first round in the political ring. When the campaign began, some friends suspected that Jack would have preferred to stay at home rather than to engage in such a treacherous contest. Now he was becoming more adept as a speaker and less anxious in crowds. He was beginning to enjoy the attention.

Grandpa Fitzgerald celebrated the victory by climbing onto a table at Kennedy headquarters and singing "Sweet Adeline," the song that during his own long and impressive political career had virtually become his theme song. Jack loved him for it.

His jubilant father turned to the person next to him and said, "I would have given odds of five thousand to one that this thing we were seeing could never have happened. I never thought Jack had it in him."

When Jack Kennedy took office as a congressman, he had the stiff, untried wings of a fledgling. He was just beginning to develop a political philosophy and had much to learn about how government works.

Jack was assigned a two-room office suite in freshman row in the old House Office Building in Washington. As he walked down the halls of Congress, Jack's boyish look prompted one colleague to mistake him for a teenager who served as a House page. He continued to dress sloppily. On the floor of the House of Representatives he would show up in wrinkled trousers and a food-spotted tie.

Despite the many invitations Jack received as a freshman congressman, he accepted very few. He preferred dining at his Georgetown home with a few friends, where he carried on the family tradition of dinner-table debates in which the problems of the world would be examined. There were certainly plenty of problems to talk about. The world had literally been torn apart by World War II.

During his three terms in Congress—Jack was reelected in 1948 and 1950—Kennedy wanted to be his own man, owing nothing to congressional party leaders. He denounced the Taft-Hartley Act, a bill aimed at placing curbs on labor unions, and he refused to sign a petition to grant clemency to James Michael Curley, the former Boston mayor who was serving a prison sentence for mail fraud.

The pale young congressman from Massachusetts did support legislation that would provide low-cost housing for the disadvantaged. When few had the courage to oppose the American Legion on anything, he publicly attacked the organization for taking a stand against the bill. On the floor of the House, he exclaimed indignantly, "The leadership of the American Legion has not had a constructive thought for the benefit of this country since 1918."

Still, Jack was plainly bored by being a congressman. He never established a niche in the U.S. House of Representatives. He found many of his colleagues uninteresting, and he also thought the rules and regulations of the House a stumbling block to action. His career as a congressman was relatively undistinguished.

In August 1947, en route to London, he stopped in Ireland to see his sister Kick (Kathleen). While visiting her he made an excursion in search of the Kennedy family in the village of New Ross, on the banks of the Barrow River in County Wexford. He had a letter from an aunt giving directions through the scattered villages of the Irish countryside to the old Kennedy family home.

At the edge of the village, in a white, thatch-roofed house with pigs and chickens scurrying around and a brood of children with hair the color of ripened corn, Jack found the family he was seeking. They offered him eggs and butter, hard to obtain in a time of postwar shortages, and Jack was touched, asking repeatedly, "What can I do for you? What can I do for you?" They wanted only one thing: that Jack drive the children—who had never been in an automobile—around the village in his station wagon. He was profoundly moved by this experience.

In London, instead of meeting his congressional colleagues, he was rushed to a hospital, suffering from acute nausea and low blood pressure. "That American friend of yours," the doctor told one family friend, "he hasn't got a year to live." He was diagnosed as having Addison's disease, a malfunction of the adrenal glands that causes nausea, weight loss, weakness, loss of appetite, and circulatory collapse. The skin takes on a brownish pigmentation, and the disease can be fatal if it is not treated promptly.

Great strides had been made in research on Addison's disease, and doctors found a successful treatment—the implantation in the body of pellets of DOCA, desoxycorticosterone acetate, a synthetic steroid hormone. When the "miracle drug" cortisone became available, Jack began to take it with DOCA and his health took a dramatic swing for the better. The Kennedys kept stores of DOCA and cortisone in safe-deposit boxes around the country so that he would always have quick access to the medicine.

The Kennedy family decided, as they had with Rosemary, to keep the illness a secret, repeatedly denying the diagnosis. Addison's disease was little understood and greatly feared by the general public, since it was usually fatal. Newspapers all carried the same story, put forth by the Kennedy family: an attack of malaria, first contracted in the South Pacific during the war, laid Congressman Kennedy low.

In May 1948, Jack had just returned from a dinner meeting and was lying on the couch when the phone rang. The call was from a *Washington Post* reporter with the news of Kathleen's death in an airplane crash in France. Jack was devastated. When he closed his eyes, he could see images of her chattering about the smallest detail of a party or speaking to him about things that mattered to both of them. Once again Jack struggled to restore an inner world shattered by loss.

In the following months he felt a measure of guilt that he was alive and that Kick and Joe, Jr., were dead. He became obsessed with death, and one day turned to his legislative aide, Timothy "Ted" Reardon. Joe, Jr.'s college roommate had followed Jack since his first congressional battle. "Tell me, Teddy boy," said Jack, "what's the best way to die?" Reardon answered that in his opinion, old age was the best way. Jack countered, "You're wrong, wrong as hell. In war—that's the best way to die. The very best way. In war."

Restless in the House of Representatives, Jack decided to run for higher office. Even before his first two-year term was over, he decided to make a bid for the governorship of Massachusetts or for a seat in the U.S. Senate. He and his staff mapped out a careful campaign strategy. They would visit every city and town in Massachusetts, and Jack would speak and shake hands. Dave Powers hung a map of the state on the bedroom wall of Kennedy's Bowdoin

Jack overcame his shyness and was learning to use television to his benefit. (1952)

Street apartment in Boston, placing pins on towns and villages where Jack had spoken.

On weekend visits to Massachusetts, Jack undertook strenuous campaign treks across the state, often involving long hours of driving on lonely mountain roads in rain and snow, to speak to people. Jack was so rushed on one occasion that he shaved in the men's room of a bowling alley. Sometimes he slept in rundown hotels. Every Friday he flew to Boston and on Sunday nights returned to Washington, D.C., by overnight sleeper train.

On his trips to Massachusetts, Jack often visited his Fitzgerald grandfather. Grandpa Honey Fitz talked about his life and shared his belief that in politics a person could make a difference. In the old man's eyes idealism and optimism still burned with phenomenal energy. "You are my namesake," Fitzgerald told his grandson one night. "You are the one to carry on our family name. And mark my word, you will walk on a far larger canvas than I."

Jack's back caused him increasing pain and he carried crutches, carefully hidden on the floor of the car. He wanted no one to see him on crutches, but away from the public Jack relied on them. His brother Bobby said, "Those who knew him well would know he was suffering only because his face was a little whiter, the lines around his eyes were a little deeper, his words a little sharper. Those who did not know him well detected nothing."

In the spring of 1952, Jack announced his candidacy for the United States Senate, running for the Democrats against popular Republican Henry Cabot Lodge, Jr. Older and more mature than Jack, a man with deep family roots in Massachusetts politics, Lodge seemed unbeatable. By the winter of 1952, the map on the Bowdoin Street wall was crowded with colored pins.

Jack's father continued to exert a tremendous influence on his political fortunes. Behind the scenes he was a manipulator and a master puppeteer. He spent enormous amounts of money on Jack's behalf. During the campaign against Lodge, one costly flyer sent to hundreds of thousands of Massachusetts families proclaimed: "John fulfills dream of brother Joe, who met death in sky over English Channel." Capitalizing on Joe, Jr.'s reputation as a war hero would ensure that the Kennedy name would be associated with patriotism, military heroism, loyalty to family and country.

If Jack was revealing some independence on the floor of the House of Representatives, he was still unable to free himself from his father's influence—and money. The elder Kennedy was both an asset and a liability to his son. He had a reputation for ruthlessness and was regarded by some as cynical and uncouth, more concerned about campaign tactics than affairs of state.

Bobby Kennedy, twenty-six years old and working as a lawyer for the U.S. Justice Department, was called in to manage the campaign. Bobby and Jack forged a bond of mutual respect and shared the same tireless energy.

The tea parties that began in the 1946 congressional election were popular. Working people rubbed shoulders with high society. Thirty-five were held during Jack's campaign against Lodge. During these teas, Rose Kennedy, surrounded by her daughters Eunice, Jean, and Pat and looking stylish and youthful, would offer a warm personal tribute to her son. Then Jack would give a brief, amiable talk and invite guests to join his family on the stage, shake hands, and

The newly elected senator celebrates his victory over the favored Republican incumbent, Henry Cabot Lodge. (1952)

have tea. Jack appealed to the maternal instinct in some of the older women, while the younger ones fell in love with the handsome young bachelor.

At one such tea, guests consumed 8,600 cups of tea or coffee. During the entire campaign, 50,000 women attended the receptions, which were unexpected and dramatic successes. When Jack beat Lodge by 70,000-plus votes, the election was called "a tea-party victory."

On January 3, 1953, a little more than two weeks before Dwight D. Eisenhower was inaugurated as president, Jack was sworn in as senator. He moved to the Senate Office Building, to Room 362, located directly opposite Vice President Richard Nixon's Senate office. In the House he had been one of four hundred thirty-five representatives, but in the Senate he was one of ninety-six. At the age of thirty-five, he had joined the ranks of the most exclusive political club in the nation. Now he could begin to make his mark.

At a Senate labor rackets committee hearing, Senator John Kennedy and his brother Robert, chief counsel to the committee, listen to a witness. (1957)

4

The Senator
(1952–1959)

One by one he subdued his father's trees

If Jack Kennedy found the work of a U.S. congressman dull, he made up for it in his time away from Capitol Hill. His quarters in Georgetown were the site of lively parties. He was widely known in Washington social circles as a ladies' man—and as the capital city's most eligible bachelor. So far, he had escaped committing himself to any one woman.

In the spring of 1952, as Kennedy was campaigning for the Senate, his father's friend Charles Bartlett, Washington correspondent for the *Chattanooga Times*, invited him to a small dinner party at his Georgetown home. There Jack was introduced to Jacqueline Bouvier. Twelve years younger than Jack, she was completing her senior year in college. One story has it that during dinner Jack leaned across the asparagus and asked her for a date.

Like Jack, Jackie Bouvier had grown up in wealth and had attended private schools. Before graduating from George Washington University, she spent two years at Vassar College and one at the Sorbonne in Paris. She was awarded the 1950 *Vogue* magazine's Prix de Paris for an article she submitted. Inclined toward the arts, she spoke French, Italian, and Spanish fluently. As the Inquiring Photographer for the *Washington Times-Herald*, she interviewed Jack as well as Richard Nixon for one of her columns.

Jackie was a woman of uncommon beauty. Her eyes were almond-shaped, her eyelashes long, her face sculptured. She spoke in a breathy whisper that some thought was an expression of her shyness; others thought it was an affectation. Her parents were divorced, and her closest friends were her father and her sister, Lee.

Jack and Jackie had an erratic courtship. While he was campaigning in Massachusetts, he called Jackie "from some oyster bar with a great clinking of coins, to ask me out to the movies the following Wednesday in Washington," she recalled. Jack was not eager to be married, but he realized that marriage was a necessity if he wanted to further his political career.

They loved books, history, and the sea, and both had a good sense of humor. They loved children. The most striking difference between the two—and it created a chasm that was never bridged—was that he was turning more and more toward the roar of the crowd, whereas she was turning away from it. She was apolitical and detested campaigning. Although she was a strong person, she wanted to please him and often deferred to him.

Jack was not a sentimental suitor; he did not shower her with flowers and gifts, although he did give her one of his favorite books, John Buchan's *Pilgrim's Way*. She dabbled in art and gave him two books that she had illustrated herself. For his benefit, she translated articles and books about Indochina from French into English.

Like his father, Jack married into a family more socially prominent than his own. Jackie was not only a Catholic but, in Joe Kennedy's words, she had "class." Next to her own father and to Jack Kennedy, Jackie would love Joe more than anybody else in the world. She was less comfortable with his mother. She seemed to annoy Rose in the same ways that Jack had irritated her when he was a boy.

One week before the wedding, Jackie asked Jack to name his best and worst qualities. He responded that irritability, impatience with the dull or mediocre, was his worst; curiosity was his best.

Cutting the cake. (1953)

On September 12, 1953, they were married by the Kennedy family friend, the Archbishop of Boston, the Most Reverend Richard J. Cushing, at St. Mary's Roman Catholic Church in Newport, Rhode Island. Close friends worried whether Jack, because of his increasing back pain, was going to be able to kneel at the altar, but he managed gracefully.

A few hours before the wedding, Jackie received a call that her father, John Vernou Bouvier III, had been drinking and was too unsteady on his feet to walk her down the aisle. Crushed, Jackie said she would not walk down the aisle without him, though in the end she changed her mind. Most guests were unaware of the humiliation and bittersweet happiness that Jackie felt on her wedding day as her stepfather, Hugh Auchincloss, walked beside her toward the altar.

Thousands of people lined the streets of Newport to catch a glimpse of the bride as her limousine drove toward the church. The reception was held at Hammersmith Farm, her stepfather's Newport estate. There were twelve bridesmaids, fifteen ushers, and a wedding cake four tiers high. Bobby was best man and toasted the couple at the wedding. Sister Pat caught the bouquet.

To the extroverted Kennedy sisters, who had welcomed Bobby's wife Ethel into the fold as one of their own, Jackie seemed fragile, genteel, and restrained. Jackie, in turn, was startled by the frenetic family activity involving both the men and the women—tennis, swimming, sailing, touch football, and parlor games. One family friend, David Hackett, wrote humorous advice in "Rules for Visiting the Kennedys": "Prepare yourself by reading the *Congressional Record, U.S. News and World Report, Time, Newsweek, Fortune, The Nation, How to Play Sneaky Tennis*, and the *Democratic Digest*. Memorize at least three good jokes. Anticipate that each Kennedy will ask you what you think of another Kennedy's (a) dress, (b) hairdo, (c) backhand, (d) latest public achievement. Be sure to answer, 'Terrific.' This should get you through dinner."

In a football huddle in Hyannis Port, Jackie asked one of Jack's friends, "Tell me one thing: Which way do I run?" It should have been no surprise to anybody when she broke her ankle playing football in one of the Kennedy family skirmishes. "Just watching them wore me out," she said.

Jackie exerted a positive influence on Jack. She not only encouraged him to eat better, but persuaded him to dress better. She had lunches sent to his Senate office in picnic baskets. For years he had paid little attention to what he ate. In her words, "he had a saltine at four in the afternoon and would get so thin."

Still, the first year of their marriage was probably one of the unhappiest years in Jack's life, and perhaps Jackie's, too. Jack's misery arose from his ongoing back pain. He was forced to use crutches constantly, and he lost an alarming amount of weight. Jackie, for her part, felt increasingly lonely. Jack

Touch football was a Kennedy family tradition at the Hyannis Port compound. (c. 1955)

placed his political life above everything and spent long hours on Capitol Hill. This left Jackie feeling even more isolated when she had a miscarriage and was advised that she would always have trouble bearing children. The realities of married life were nowhere near as glamorous as the splashy Newport wedding.

In the Senate, however, Jack felt more and more at ease. Although he had relatively little impact in his first years as a senator, he enjoyed being close to the center of power. Because he took few strong positions, he offended few of his colleagues, and his engaging manner made him a favorite on Capitol Hill.

Jack's desk, in perpetual disarray, was always piled high with papers, "as if someone had taken a wastepaper basket and turned it upside down," his secretary, Evelyn Lincoln, said. He would scribble telephone numbers on small pieces of paper, stuffing them into his pockets and into his wallet, unable to find them later. He could take a nap at the drop of a hat. He was like an absentminded professor, leaving his briefcase or overcoat in a hotel closet, restaurant, or airplane. Muggsey O'Leary, his faithful driver and right-hand man, made many hair-raising last-minute trips to the airport. When Jack was behind the wheel the drive was even more dangerous, for he drove perilously fast.

To the annoyance of his friends, his old habit of never carrying money followed him to the Senate. It was not as if he hoarded money. On the contrary, as a congressman and a senator he donated his government salaries to charity, and he was grateful that his father's wealth made his own financial position secure. Joe Kennedy had bestowed a million-dollar trust fund upon each of his children, so Jack was able to pursue his political career without worrying about how to support himself. He didn't have to be concerned about where his next meal was coming from, nor was he consumed with the desire to acquire more money or to build a financial empire.

Jack Kennedy paid a price, however, for living on his father's money. At a crucial moment Joe Kennedy's influence prevented the young senator from taking a strong stand, when justice and the national interest would have been served by forthrightness and courage.

The year was 1954, and Joseph McCarthy was terrorizing the country. A Wisconsin Republican at the summit of his political career, Senator McCarthy was making indiscriminate, unfounded, and reckless charges against individuals and groups, accusing them of being either Communists or "Communist sympathizers." Americans had long been uneasy about communism, a system in which the community or state, rather than the individual, owns all property. The increasing power of the Soviet Union, whose leaders proclaimed that the whole world would eventually embrace communism, worried many people in the United States. Since the end of World War II, the United States and the Soviet Union had mistrusted and feared each other. Although no physical conflict had broken out, the battle of social and political ideas was so strong that it came to be known as the Cold War.

Joseph McCarthy, as chairman of the Senate Permanent Subcommittee on Investigations, and members of the House Un-American Activities Committee were playing on these fears. Although Americans had a constitutional right to express their political opinions, McCarthy labeled Communists and those he considered sympathetic to communism as traitors to the "American way of life." Eventually, it did not matter to McCarthy whether or not he could prove that his targets had any real links to communism. He made his charges indiscriminately, ruining the lives and careers of many citizens. In this witch-hunt atmosphere, McCarthy's congressional colleagues were forced to take sides, either by going along with McCarthy's ruthless inquiries or by speaking against them.

Joe Kennedy, long suspicious of the Communists, was friendly with McCarthy. Jack knew and liked McCarthy, too, and for a time Bobby Kennedy had served as assistant counsel to McCarthy's Senate subcommittee. The main job of the subcommittee was to report on subversive activities affecting the United States government. Eunice Kennedy had also dated Senator McCarthy.

Jack had done his best to distance himself from the issue, trying to avoid it. Massachusetts had a higher proportion of McCarthy supporters than any other state, and Jack did not want to lose voters. McCarthy was a powerful and intimidating political force. Nor was Jack eager to side against his father. Jack took issue with McCarthy only when his practices were clearly illegal.

During 1953 McCarthy's "red-baiting" went virtually unchallenged, but by 1954 the outrageousness of his tactics caused a backlash. A motion to censure McCarthy came to the Senate floor. While many of his fellow Democrats made it clear that they would now stand up to McCarthy, Jack Kennedy remained silent. The spell of his father's opinion apparently paralyzed him.

As it turned out, Jack was spared the agony of voting on the measure. On December 2, 1954, when the motion to censure was passed in the Senate, he was in the Hospital for Special Surgery in New York, struggling to recover from a dangerous operation. Several doctors had been opposed to the spinal fusion, fearing that his Addison's disease would complicate his recovery and that infection might set in. They told him he had only a fifty-fifty chance of waking up from the anesthesia. But Jack was adamant. "I'd rather be dead," he said, pointing to his crutches, "than spend the rest of my life on these things."

Infection did set in. Jack was placed on the critical list, and his doctors did not expect him to survive. He was so close to death that he was given the last rites of the Catholic Church. With Jackie's help he rallied enough to be taken to his Palm Beach home for the Christmas holidays. He was depressed and as low as he had ever been. His friend Lem Billings said later, "We came close to losing him. I don't just mean losing his life. I mean losing him as a person." Within four months he was back in the hospital for a second operation.

The second operation was more successful, and Jackie, Dave Powers, and brother Teddy accompanied Jack back to Palm Beach. He spent months recuperating, with Jackie at his side almost day and night. She read to him, recited poems from memory, and dug up books at old bookstores that would distract him from the pain. She taught him how to paint.

Long before his operation, Jack had been writing magazine articles on issues of the day. During that time he became fascinated by the integrity of John Quincy Adams, who upheld his beliefs despite the pressures of his constituents. What started as a magazine article became the book *Profiles in Courage*. He wrote about eight leaders of Congress who had showed the courage of their convictions by upholding them at great political risk. Jack was consumed by the project during his recuperation.

A board was propped up in front of him and he wrote while lying flat on his back. He dictated some of the material into a recording machine. Cartons of books were sent to him from the Library of Congress. When Jack was too exhausted to write or read, Jackie and Dave Powers would read to him.

As the days went by, Jack gained strength, first walking the agonizing fifty feet from his room to a chair beside the swimming pool and later walking the distance to the beach. Jack's father confided to Dave Powers as he watched Jack grow in strength: "I know nothing can happen to him now because I've stood by his deathbed three times, and each time I said good-bye to him, and each time he came back stronger." Seven months after his first operation he was back on the Senate floor.

Profiles in Courage describes the kind of political bravery that Jack Kennedy had not demonstrated when Joseph McCarthy was terrorizing the nation. Writing the book served as a catharsis—a cleansing or purging of guilt—for his own lack of courage in relation to the McCarthy issue. It soothed any misgivings he had about not standing up to Joe McCarthy. It gave him a way of investigating the nature of moral courage. Jack had proved his physical courage in war and he had proved he could endure pain stoically and with humor. But moral courage provided another kind of challenge.

Published January 1, 1956, the book became a best-seller and won the 1957 Pulitzer Prize for biography. Jack was elated. He contributed the $500 prize to the United Negro College Fund. He was quite upset—more upset than his close friends ever remember him being—when it was suggested that he, in

John Kennedy lived with constant back pain. He often relied on crutches, as he did here at a campaign appearance with his mother. (1952)

fact, was not the author of the book. Kennedy threatened to take legal action against his accusers—and opened the original manuscript and drafts to public scrutiny, thus helping to allay doubts of authorship.*

As the 1956 Democratic convention approached, Jack often heard his name mentioned as a possible vice-presidential candidate. The party's nominee for

---

*Jack's Senate staff members, especially Ted Sorensen, did assist him in the research and writing, but it was not unusual for a political figure to obtain help with speeches and even books. While it is true that Kennedy received the sole credit for a work that was in part a group effort, Jack's talent with words remains undisputed. Many of the book's best features are the result of his immersion in writing during several months of convalescence. *Profiles in Courage* was essentially his own.

president was the eloquent and intellectual Adlai Stevenson, one of the founders of the United Nations.

The convention was the first in which television played an instrumental role, and Jack came across well. He was photogenic, energetic, and appealing. Still, Kennedy lost the vice-presidential bid to Senator Estes Kefauver.

"Blue language flashed all over the room," said presidential aide Kenny O'Donnell when Bobby placed a call to his dad in France to let him know what had happened. "Whew!" said Bobby. "Is he mad!" Joe Kennedy was convinced that the loss would be a grave blow to Jack's growing prestige. He was sure that the family's Catholicism would be blamed. Nonetheless, Jack had begun to pave his own way. In the defeat he had realized a great political triumph: He was now recognized throughout the country as a potential national leader. In addition, he had reached a personal milestone: He had decided to seek the vice-presidential nomination despite his father's advice to the contrary, and his decision proved correct.

Consuming political ambitions distracted him from his family life. At the time of the 1956 convention, Jackie was pregnant and particularly anxious, remembering the miscarriage in the first year of their marriage. Although she accompanied him to Chicago for the convention, politics totally preoccupied Jack and he barely saw her the entire week. After the convention, Jackie went to Newport to await their baby. Jack, exhausted, headed for a visit with his father on the French Riviera.

Jackie begged Jack not to go, but he went anyway. She was upset and bitter. A few days after her arrival in Newport, Jackie was rushed to the hospital, where she gave birth by emergency cesarean operation to a stillborn baby girl. Jackie was in critical condition. The Kennedy family tried to reach Jack; but with his father's blessings, he had joined Senator George Smathers and brother Teddy aboard a chartered yacht. He was not aware of what had taken place until he called home three days after his child's death. The front page of the *Washington Post* carried the headline "Senator Kennedy on Mediterranean Trip Unaware His Wife Has Lost Baby."

Deeply hurt, Jackie learned ways of coping with Jack's irresponsibility and apparent indifference. The Kennedys moved out of Hickory Hill, the Virginia house they had bought, where Jackie had decorated a nursery for the baby. She blamed the hectic pace of campaigning for the loss of her child and sought greater privacy. In Hyannis Port she insisted that she and Jack eat dinner by themselves, instead of with his family.

Jack, however, was rapidly gaining national attention, and rather than slowing down, his pace quickened. Soon after the 1956 convention, Jack said to Dave Powers: "If I work hard for four years, I ought to be able to pick up all the marbles." He was referring to a bid for the presidency. Nearly five hundred speaking invitations a week poured into his office. In 1957 he gave one hundred and fifty talks across the country; in 1958 he gave more.

His youth, vigor, wealth, and family made him a desirable subject for newspaper and magazine articles. An article in *McCall's* entitled "The Senator Is in a Hurry" quoted his father as saying, "I got Jack into politics—I was the one. I told him Joe was dead and that it was therefore his responsibility to run for Congress. He didn't want to. He felt he didn't have the ability and he still feels that way. But I told him he had to." If Jack still felt incapable, it was not visible. His confidence was soaring.

Nineteen fifty-seven was an eventful year for another reason—on the day after Thanksgiving Jackie gave birth to a healthy seven-pound-two-ounce girl, Caroline Bouvier Kennedy, who was christened at St. Patrick's Cathedral in New York City on December 13. Jack choked up when he told the news to Lem Billings. For both parents the child was a "gift outright."

In Congress, Jack was active on the Senate labor racketeering committee during the heated and angry investigations into corruption in the nation's big labor unions. Since the unions were traditionally big supporters of the Democratic party, it took some courage for Kennedy to take a leading role in the investigation. Robert Kennedy served as counsel to the committee, and both brothers confronted the corrupt leaders, including the powerful Teamsters Union chief, Jimmy Hoffa.

In his years in the Senate, Jack matured as a campaigner and as a states-man. He began to recognize politics as an art. In answer to one comment about his youth, Jack replied, "Youth is not a presumption of vitality or old age a presumption of wisdom. . . . It's the quality of the individual that matters." He continued to understate his strengths. He was a World War II hero, he said, because he had no choice: "They sank my boat."

During his years in Congress, Jack Kennedy had developed as a politician and a leader. His political philosophy, almost nonexistent in 1946 when he began his political career, now embraced self-restraint, moderation, and prudence. He became increasingly liberal in his views. His early years, he once commented, were a reflection of the fact that he had "just come out of [his] father's house," one that was conservative in outlook. He moved away from militarism toward negotiation. World peace became a compulsion.

Jack continued to be restless. One interviewer recommended that Jack read Nostradamus, the sixteenth-century French astrologer and physician, to see what the future might hold. Jack answered quickly in his clear, precise tone, "It's better not to know."

In 1958 Kennedy won a smashing reelection to the Senate, with more than seventy percent of the Massachusetts vote. His overwhelming victory—the widest margin any candidate had ever received in Massachusetts—prodded his ambition and strengthened his decision to seek the presidency in 1960.

President Eisenhower welcomes President-elect Kennedy to a meeting at the White House. (December 1960)

5

Taking Command
(1960–1961)

Then he flung outward, feet first, with a swish

On January 2, 1960, John F. Kennedy, forty-two years of age, told the American people that he wanted to be their president.

He faced serious obstacles. Many people thought him too young and too inexperienced to aspire to the White House. Dwight Eisenhower was a popular president, and his popularity would give any Republican the advantage in the general election. And Kennedy was a Catholic in a predominantly Protestant country.

Of course, Jack Kennedy had significant advantages as well. He had the good fortune *not* to be on the losing Democratic party ticket in 1956, and he used the four years preparing for his own race for the White House. Thanks to his father's money, he flew around the country in his private plane, the *Caroline*, introducing himself to voters and to state and local politicians. He built a wide power base. And inside the Kennedy family, Jack had a small army of reliable, enthusiastic campaign workers.

The first key test was the Democratic party primary in Wisconsin. Longtime Minnesota senator Hubert Humphrey emerged as Kennedy's main rival for the nomination. If Kennedy could beat Humphrey in Wisconsin, it would send a signal that the young senator from Massachusetts would be a strong candidate.

Bobby Kennedy marshaled the troops and blanketed Wisconsin with Kennedys. Jackie walked the frozen streets with her husband. Jack's sisters Eunice and Pat were on the scene, and his youngest brother, Teddy, spent as much time as he could before rushing back to Massachusetts for the birth of his first child.

Kennedy did defeat Humphrey in Wisconsin, but the victory was not impressive. He won six of the state's ten congressional districts, with a stronger showing in the heavily Catholic cities than in the rural Protestant areas. Watching the returns in his hotel suite, Kennedy flicked off the television in disgust as the anchorman described the "religious dilemma."

During the twentieth century, Roman Catholics had gained importance in the mainstream of United States politics. But Joe Kennedy had warned his son that religion would be a major issue in the campaign. Only once before, in 1928, had a Catholic been nominated for president by a major party. That candidate, Governor Al Smith of New York, had been soundly defeated by Herbert Hoover. Although there were many possible explanations for Hoover's victory, many people thought that Smith's religion kept him from winning. Even in 1960 some people worried that a Catholic president would take orders from the Pope. During the Democratic primaries, Kennedy had to decide how to handle this "religious dilemma." Should he take the high road and insist that religion ought not be a matter for political discussion? Or should he meet the issue head-on?

In West Virginia, a state that was almost entirely Protestant, Jack chose to discuss his Catholicism freely and frankly. There he sounded a note that would be an important part of his campaign theme right into the fall. He emphasized his commitment to the absolute separation of church and state: "For while this year it may be a Catholic against whom the finger of suspicion is pointed, in other years it has been, and may someday be again, a Jew—or a

Quaker—or a Unitarian—or a Baptist. . . . Today I may be the victim—but tomorrow it may be you—until the whole fabric of our harmonious society is ripped apart at a time of great national peril."

On May 10, 1960, the voters of West Virginia went to the polls and gave John Kennedy a solid victory. With that win, Kennedy was established as a national candidate. He had proved that he could win outside New England and that he could win the votes of Protestants.

As the campaign wore on, Jack learned how to make the best use of reporters. Throughout most of the history of the United States, presidential candidates had scarcely campaigned at all. It was considered undignified to go before the people and beg for votes, and the distances were immense. In the twentieth century, candidates faced the people more regularly. The rise of radio and then television made good relations with the press essential for anyone running for office in 1960.

Kennedy liked reporters. He had done a short stint as a journalist himself, and he happily invited members of the press aboard his plane to chat and banter as he traveled around the country. In return, however, Kennedy expected favorable coverage from the media. After all, his looks were one of his greatest assets. He also had a glamorous wife and an appealing three-year-old daughter. Good pictures could help win the favor of the voters. But he was concerned that they be the right pictures. The photographers for the major magazines wanted to catch the public's eye. They wanted something unusual, something personal, like a picture of the candidate in a funny hat, or a posed shot of Jack Kennedy munching on a hot dog, pizza, or knish—photos that linked him to the "common" person.

Kennedy knew that the photographers had their job to do, but he was determined not to let them catch him in any pose that did not look "presidential." No funny hats; and above all, no photographs of the candidate eating. It was too easy to look silly. "After all," he told one photographer, "there are a lot of clods carrying cameras in this country."

By June 1960, it was clear that Jack Kennedy was the favorite to win the

On the campaign trail in the key state of West Virginia. Kennedy's triumph there helped allay doubts about his ability to win the support of Protestant voters. (1960)

Democratic party's nomination at the Los Angeles convention in July. He had soundly defeated Hubert Humphrey in the primaries, and the other candidates could show only regional support.

Yet the nomination was not locked up. Many convention delegates are not chosen directly by voters through the primary system. Instead, they are hand-picked by politicians and other leaders of the Democratic party in the various states. Many of these delegates in 1960 were suspicious of the young, untraditional senator from Massachusetts.

Behind the scenes, one very powerful man, Lyndon Baines Johnson of Texas, was working hard to fuel an atmosphere of distrust. The majority leader of the Senate, Johnson had not run in any of the primaries, but he had a burning desire to be president of the United States. Perhaps there were enough suspicions in the air to topple Jack Kennedy. If so, Lyndon Johnson was ready.

Johnson and Kennedy had served in the Senate together for eight years. Although they belonged to the same party and supported many of the same causes, they had little love for each other. Johnson, who referred to Jack Kennedy as "that skinny son-of-a-bitch," disliked his colleague's cool charm and envied his easy public posture. He thought Kennedy had done nothing of importance in the Senate, though "he looked awfully good on the goddamn television screen." Kennedy, for his part, looked down on Johnson's coarse southwestern manner.

In the frenzy of the Democratic National Convention, Johnson pulled out all the stops to try to prevent Kennedy from winning the nomination on the first ballot. Kennedy needed more than half the delegates present to vote for him to gain a victory. Johnson thought that if Kennedy did not win a majority on the first ballot, delegates would have some doubts about his ability to win against the Republicans in the fall. He hoped that the convention would turn to a powerful, well-known politician who knew the ins and outs of party politics: the majority leader himself.

All week long Kennedy and his staff fought brushfires. They had to quash stories spread by the Johnson staff that Jack Kennedy suffered from Addison's disease. (The gossip, of course, was true, but the Kennedy advisors knew that if they did not deny it, delegates might have doubts about their man's fitness for the job.) Kennedy's people had to play down a noisy demonstration for Adlai Stevenson of Illinois, the unsuccessful Democratic candidate in 1952 and 1956. Above all, they worked to convince uneasy delegates not to remain uncommitted on the first ballot.

Right down to the day of the actual balloting, Kennedy and his staff scrambled for votes. By tradition, the ballots are called alphabetically by state. Not until the state of Wyoming cast its fifteen ballots for John Fitzgerald Kennedy was the nomination secure.

Kennedy could not bask in the glory of this triumph for long. His first major decision was already upon him. Whom should he ask to be his running mate, the vice-presidential candidate on the ticket? Jack batted around ideas with Bobby Kennedy. They needed balance: someone who represented a different part of the country, a different political philosophy, someone who might appeal to more conservative voters who would distrust a candidate perceived as a Massachusetts liberal.

In an astute maneuver, Kennedy turned to, of all people, Lyndon Johnson. He disliked Johnson personally, but the majority leader had shown he had strong support at the convention. He certainly presented a contrast, and he might help Kennedy capture Johnson's home state of Texas, a crucial prize. Besides, Kennedy assumed that Johnson would not accept the position. The majority leader wielded much more power in his present position than he would in the largely ceremonial role of vice president. Kennedy aimed to flatter Johnson by doing him the courtesy of inviting him to be on the ticket. That would curry Johnson's favor while leaving him free to choose a more congenial running mate.

To Kennedy's surprise, Johnson accepted. On his path to what Kennedy would call the New Frontier, the Irish Catholic senator from Massachusetts would be accompanied by a man born and bred in the Old Frontier of southwest Texas. Kennedy's political gambit backfired.

"It is time for a new generation of leadership," John F. Kennedy told the convention when he accepted the nomination on the night of July 15. "All over the world, particularly in the newer nations, young men are coming to power, men who are not bound by the traditions of the past, men who are not blinded by the old fears and hate and rivalries, men who can cast off the old slogans and the old delusions. I'm asking each of you to be pioneers toward that New Frontier."

It was an eloquent speech, and heralded a different kind of political campaign. Other men could run on their experience, on their long years of service, on their party loyalty. Jack Kennedy emphasized his youth, with a vision that looked toward the future. The idea of the New Frontier also reflected

Lyndon Baines Johnson campaigning at the Boston Common. (1960)

the past. It reminded listeners of the colonists who had settled the continent and tamed the wilderness. Too, it echoed Franklin Delano Roosevelt's New Deal, the ambitious Democratic program that helped the United States weather the Great Depression. Jack Kennedy wanted to have it both ways. He wanted to offer himself as bold, young, and different, but he also wanted voters to think of him as continuing the historic tradition.

Less than two weeks after Kennedy's acceptance speech, the Republican party chose Vice President Richard M. Nixon as its nominee. Nixon, in his turn, selected as his running mate Henry Cabot Lodge, Jr., of Massachusetts, whom Kennedy had defeated in his first senate race in 1952. The stage was set for one of the most hotly contested general election campaigns in U.S. history.

At first glance, the two presidential candidates presented a contrast. Kennedy represented the East; Nixon, raised in California, the West. Kennedy was schooled in the Ivy League; Nixon at a small Quaker college. Kennedy was handsome, charming, accessible; Nixon was jowly and abrasive, with a history of "dirty politics." Kennedy asserted the traditional Democratic position that government should take an active role in righting wrongs and helping the needy; Nixon, as a Republican, was more inclined to call for government to "get off the back" of the people.

Yet in 1960 many people did not see a great difference between the two. Both were eager to reach voters at the center of the political spectrum. As a result, they both sounded very much alike on many of the key questions of the day.

In foreign policy, the most important issue of the campaign was the relationship between the United States and the Soviet Union. Kennedy and Nixon both made strong statements opposing the spread of communism. Each tried to argue that he was the man who would be better able to "stand up to the Russians."

On the important issue of civil rights for blacks, both candidates tried to straddle the center. They talked in general terms about political and social equality, without making strong statements that might alienate white voters. The civil rights issue, however, made it clear that the two were not cut from the same cloth. The difference between Nixon and Kennedy may have come down more to personality than to ideas, but that difference was crucial.

One key incident put the candidates to the test. On October 16, 1960, Dr. Martin Luther King, Jr., and thirty-five college students were arrested in Atlanta, Georgia, for protesting segregation at a downtown department store. The students were released, but King was jailed.

Although he was not tall, King had a commanding presence. He had been born in Atlanta, where he and his father had served as copastors of the Ebenezer Baptist Church. King preached that nonviolent resistance—protest marches, sit-ins, demonstrations—was the most powerful weapon available to blacks in their struggle against injustice. While living in Montgomery, Alabama, in 1955, he had helped lead a year-long boycott that won for blacks the right to sit wherever they chose on city buses. Like Kennedy, King had a magnetic personality. He was an eloquent and controversial speaker who made passionate appeals to the conscience of white Americans and inspired his black followers to seek justice and equality.

In the South, where laws discriminating against blacks were most widespread, white officials frequently tried to put a stop to civil-rights activism by finding phony reasons for arresting the movement's leaders. After Martin Luther King's arrest in 1960, he was sentenced to a term at hard labor on a trumped-up charge related to an earlier traffic violation. He was moved from jail to jail around Georgia. This shuttling frightened his followers, who knew that no black man, not even a world-famous civil rights leader, was safe in the prison system of a southern state.

At first the Kennedy campaign tried to duck the issue of the King arrest. Civil rights leaders pushed both parties for statements of support, but with just over three weeks until the election, neither presidential candidate wanted to risk losing white votes by making a bold public statement. Kennedy spoke privately to the governor of Georgia, who promised the senator that he would help "get the son of a bitch out of jail" if Kennedy would make no statements about the case. "I agreed," Kennedy told his civil rights aide, Harris Wofford. "What we want most is to get King out, isn't it?"

But Wofford wanted more. He wanted Kennedy to speak out against the treatment King was receiving. Otherwise, law enforcement officials in the southern states would be able to take such actions repeatedly.

On October 26, Wofford urged Sargent Shriver, Kennedy's brother-in-law, to try to convince Jack to make a simple gesture of support for a man unfairly imprisoned. The candidate was in Chicago with his brother Bobby and top advisors Ted Sorensen and Kenny O'Donnell, among others. These aides, es-

Martin Luther King, Jr., at Boston University. (September 1964)

pecially Bobby, were adamantly against Jack's involving himself in what they considered a no-win situation. Shriver waited until the rest of the men were out of the room, and then he reminded Jack about the "lousy treatment" King was receiving in jail. He added that Coretta Scott King, the jailed leader's wife, was expecting a baby and was herself under considerable stress.

"I think you ought to give her a call, Jack," Shriver suggested.

"What the hell," Jack responded. "That's a decent thing to do. Why not? Get her on the phone."

The call was brief. Kennedy told Mrs. King: "I just wanted you to know that I was thinking about you and Dr. King," and made an offer of help. Coretta King said that she appreciated his concern. And that was all.

The phone call was a middle ground, typical of John Kennedy. It was neither the bold, impassioned statement against racism nor the plea for justice that civil rights leaders wanted. But the call was preferable to Richard Nixon's silence.

When he learned of it, Bobby Kennedy was furious—even though he had made a highly unethical private call to berate the judge who was holding

King in jail. He was unhappy that Jack had acted without consulting him, but he was determined to make the best of a bad situation. Still worried about backlash among whites, Bobby and other members of the staff did their best to keep the story of the message to Mrs. King out of the white press, and they succeeded fairly well. At the same time, they made sure that word of the call leaked out where it might help them—in the black community.

When King was released two days later, he expressed his gratitude to Kennedy but declined to endorse his candidacy. However, King's father, Martin Luther King, Sr., himself a powerful Baptist minister, announced that he was switching his allegiance from Nixon to Kennedy. He promised that he could deliver a "suitcase of votes" for the Democrats. "I had expected to vote against Senator Kennedy because of his religion," "Daddy" King told his supporters, "but now he can be my president, Catholic or whatever he is."

Jack Kennedy, grateful for the support, was amused by Daddy King's remarks about his Catholicism: "That was a hell of a bigoted statement," Kennedy told Harris Wofford. "Imagine Martin Luther King having a bigot for a father." He paused, grinning, and added, "Well, we all have fathers, don't we?"

The call to Coretta King gave Kennedy a tremendous boost in the black community. But he made his appeal to the majority of voters through television. In front of the cameras, Richard Nixon could not match Jack Kennedy. The vice president tried to emphasize his own "experience" at the expense of his opponent's youth, but that strategy could not compete with Kennedy's self-assured energy. The candidates met for four debates on national television. Many people who heard the debates on the radio thought that they had performed equally well, or even that Nixon sounded better. But the vast majority of prospective voters watched the debates on television, where the crude lighting brought out sinister shadows on Nixon's features. Jack Kennedy's appearance put people at ease and helped voters overcome their objections to his youth, his Catholicism, and his wealth.

At last, on November 8, 1960, the people went to the polls. Candidate Ken-

John and Jacqueline Kennedy after voting in the presidential election. (November 1960)

nedy, anxious and exhausted, spent the day in Hyannis Port, where he did his best to find something to do. Bobby and his lieutenants spent the day on the phones, making sure the Democrats voted, nervously monitoring reports from poll watchers around the country. Jack had breakfast with the family, chatted with his father, drummed up a game of touch football, stopped in briefly at Bobby's command center. Patience was never Jack Kennedy's strong suit. Across the land millions of people lined up to decide his fate, and there was no longer anything that he could do.

If the day was long, the night was longer still. At midnight, the election was still in doubt. Early returns reflected a Democratic surge in the East and the big cities, but as returns came in from the outlying parts of the country,

Nixon was forging ahead. As Tuesday turned to Wednesday and the returns trickled in during the early morning hours, the excitement in Hyannis Port turned to anxiety. Four key states—Minnesota, Illinois, Michigan, and California—were still in doubt. If two of those states went to Nixon, the months of effort and exhaustion would have been in vain.

By 3:00 A.M., Kennedy appeared to have 262 electoral votes locked up, but he was still 8 votes shy of victory. The networks, bold with their predictions earlier in the evening, were suddenly unsure. It was a seesaw contest. It could go either way.

There was nothing more he could do, and he was tired of waiting. With his own future, with the nation's future, hanging in the balance, Jack Kennedy left the command center, walked across the Hyannis Port lawn, and went to bed, still not knowing whether or not he had been elected president of the United States.

Three hours later, Ted Sorensen brought him news: He was over the top. It was a victory by the slimmest of margins. Out of almost 69 million voters across the nation, only 120,000 more had voted for John Kennedy than for Richard Nixon. If 5,000 Democratic votes in Illinois and 12,000 in Minnesota had been cast for Republicans, Richard Nixon would have been elected the thirty-fifth president. Although the nation was deeply divided, Jack Kennedy had won the election.

Jack made his way to the Hyannis Armory, where hundreds of reporters awaited the first public remarks by the president-elect. The man they saw was not the energetic campaigner of the first part of the year. He was not given to public celebration. He had taken to heart Joe Kennedy's premium on winning, but he could not yet savor the victory. For Jack Kennedy, the aspect of politics he was best at—the political contest itself—was over. He had always been better at running for office than at performing his work as a congressman or senator. Now, somehow, he would have to learn how to govern.

His face was puffy from lack of sleep, his voice lacked the intensity of his finest public appearances. But a flash of charm, that willingness to connect the public with the private moment, stayed with him. Toward the end of his brief statement, he glanced at Jackie, eight months pregnant and standing beside him, and then he looked back toward the reporters and the cameras. "Today," he said, "we begin to prepare for a new administration—and a new baby."

The new baby arrived before the new administration. On Thanksgiving Day, 1960, Jacqueline Kennedy, again without her husband, was in the throes of childbirth in her Georgetown home with Caroline and her nanny, Maud Shaw. The baby was not due until late December, and Jackie was in pain and frightened. "Can you come quickly, Miss Shaw?" she called.

The president-elect, en route to Florida aboard his private plane, received an urgent radio message. It seemed that only moments before, he had been enjoying Thanksgiving dinner with his family, but now his wife had been rushed by ambulance to Georgetown University Hospital. He was worried and conscience-stricken, knowing that the pregnancy had been lonely for her and that the birth could be still lonelier. Kennedy chided himself that he was never at her side when she needed him.

When the plane touched down in Palm Beach, the president-elect transferred to a faster plane to return to Washington. On the way home word came that Jackie had given birth to a healthy six-pound three-ounce boy and that she was fine. The press correspondents applauded and cheered. The president-elect, noticeably relieved, stood up and bowed ceremoniously, then resumed his seat. Exuberant, he lit up one of his favorite cigars and went back to the work of selecting a cabinet for his administration.

"Name that boy Lyndon Johnson and a heifer calf will be his," wrote the vice president—elect in a telegram. But the baby was christened John Fitzgerald Kennedy, Jr., later known to the public as "John-John." He was Jack Kennedy's second living child, his first son, and the eighteenth grandchild of Rose and Joe Kennedy.

Concerned about his inaugural address, Kennedy asked Ted Sorensen to try to put his finger on the reason for the great success of Abraham Lincoln's Gettysburg Address. After studying Lincoln's speeches, Sorensen reported that he never used a two- or three-syllable word where a one-syllable word would do, and he never used two or three words where one would do.

Kennedy wanted to keep the speech short. "I don't want people to think I'm a windbag," he told Sorensen. As with all his speeches, Kennedy had a team of gifted writers who worked on the early drafts—and who composed many of the president's most memorable lines. Kennedy himself played a large part in molding, shaping, and reworking versions. Even on the morning of his inauguration he was penciling in changes on the typed draft of his address.

On January 19, 1961, the eve of the inauguration, there was a heightened sense of excitement in Washington, D.C. Snow, a rare and welcome sight in the southern climate of the nation's capital, began to fall late in the day. By evening it blanketed the city. Drivers skidded and abandoned their cars in drifts, but all in all, the sudden storm created an atmosphere of festivity.

Throughout the night a crew of thousands, some with torch blowers, cleared the eight-mile parade route from the White House to the Capitol. The morning dawned cold and crisply clear. Kennedy attended an 8:00 A.M. mass at a Georgetown church, where he noticed his mother alone in prayer. He and Jackie had coffee with President and Mrs. Eisenhower and drove with them in the bubble-top limousine to the Capitol.

At 12:22 P.M., the ceremony began with a lengthy invocation by Cardinal Richard Cushing. Contralto Marian Anderson stepped forward and sang "The Star-Spangled Banner" in rich, triumphant tones.

Poet Robert Frost, old and slightly bent, his white hair a match for the new snow, was more concerned about the gusts of wind and glare of the sun than the smoke from short-circuited electric wires beneath the lectern. He struggled to read the first three lines of the poem that he had written for the occasion:

> Summoning artists to participate
> In the august occasions of the state
> Seems something artists ought to celebrate—

Then he called out that he couldn't see the words. The glare was blinding him. Vice President–elect Lyndon Johnson quickly came to his assistance, using his top hat to shield him. But the poet, instead of reading the new composition, recited from memory his classic poem "The Gift Outright."

Without topcoat or hat on that blustery, cold day, John Fitzgerald Kennedy, his hand on Grandfather Honey Fitz's Bible, was sworn in at 12:51 P.M. as the thirty-fifth president of the United States. Immediately following the oath, President Kennedy's youthful voice, strong and firm, rang out with the words of his inaugural address: "Let the word go forth from this time and place, to friend and foe alike, that the torch has been passed to a new gen-

Chief Justice Earl Warren administers the oath of office to the new president. (January 20, 1960)

eration of Americans." He sounded a call for the power of unity over division and of reconciliation over confrontation.

Seconds after the speech, amid rousing applause, President Kennedy's predecessor, in a hearty gesture, reached out his hand and exclaimed, "You're it now, boy." Dwight David Eisenhower had been the oldest man ever to hold the office of president of the United States; John Fitzgerald Kennedy became the youngest president-elect.

For forty-three-year-old Kennedy, the first U.S. president born in the twentieth century and the first Roman Catholic president in the history of the nation, the moment was one of exhilarating triumph. Although things had not worked out exactly as his father had expected, the family dream was fulfilled. Despite his early shyness and hesitancy, his relentless back pain and poor health, and his uneasiness about entering the world of politics, Jack had at last stepped out of his brother's shadow. In Ireland, where the first Kennedy had begun his journey to the United States more than a century earlier, bonfires were being lighted. And in the eyes of John Fitzgerald Kennedy's father, sitting on the rostrum behind the president, tears were visible.

In the evening, after the parade, the president and the First Lady attended lavish inaugural balls. Late in the night, Jacqueline "just crumpled" and retired to the White House, while her husband joined friends at parties until the early hours of the morning.

In the freezing predawn hours, the president paused on the steps of the White House. He turned to his small circle of friends to nod good-bye and to acknowledge the glorious day. It had been the high point in his life, the climax of a journey that had held no assurance of victory. The serious daring had begun some time before with the death of Joe, Jr., with the urging of his father, and with the words of his grandpa Fitzgerald: "You will walk a larger canvas than I." Alone, John Fitzgerald Kennedy stepped vigorously through the open doors into the White House.

The president meets with a delegation of civil rights leaders from the National Association for the Advancement of Colored People. (summer 1961)

6

The Fires of Frustration
(1961–1963)

Truth broke in
With all her matter-of-fact about the ice storm

On the day that John F. Kennedy gave his inaugural address on the steps of the Capitol, a young man in Jackson, Mississippi, listened carefully. James Meredith heard the new president proclaim Thomas Jefferson's belief that the rights of man come not from the generosity of the state but from the hand of God. The twenty-nine-year-old veteran of the United States Air Force decided that Kennedy's words offered him the chance to pursue a dream. The next day he wrote to the admissions office at the University of Mississippi for an application.

It was, perhaps, a small thing to do for his country. After all, in 1961 hundreds of thousands of other United States citizens applied to college. But James Meredith's case was different. Meredith was an African American. In the 113-year history of "Ole Miss," the tax-supported university had never knowingly accepted a black man or woman. James Meredith knew that he would not be able to attend without a fight. Discrimination in public schools and colleges on the basis of race had been ruled unconstitutional by the United States Supreme Court in *Brown* v. *Board of Education* in 1954, but school systems and universities throughout the land disregarded the order. Meredith needed the United States government and the new president on his side.

But how much was John Kennedy willing to do to help black Americans? In his speeches he had a great deal to say about the "rights of man" but little about the lives of millions of black citizens of the United States.

In 1961, almost a century after the end of the Civil War, there were still many areas of the country where whites and blacks had to drink from separate water fountains. A black traveler might drive hundreds of miles without finding a motel willing to rent him a room for the night. In many places, a white man could still kill a black man, brag about it, and be judged "not guilty" by an all-white jury.

It was not just in the South. In northern cities such as John Kennedy's hometown of Boston, whites used tricks and stalling tactics to continue the practice of school segregation—keeping white children and black children in separate classrooms, even separate buildings. Black children were frequently assigned to schools with crumbling ceilings, rats in the hallways, and worn-out textbooks. There were still many laws on the books that kept blacks from voting, from equal opportunities in work and housing, and from enjoying basic human dignity; and those laws that did protect the civil rights of blacks were frequently ignored. Black Americans were increasingly angry about these injustices, but few whites in politics truly understood the depth of their desperation.

Jack Kennedy had little experience with black issues and scarcely any black friends. There simply had not been many walking the tree-lined streets of Brookline or the halls of Choate. Even the navy, during World War II, kept blacks and whites in separate companies. During the presidential campaign he admitted to one aide, "You know, I'm way behind on this, because I've hardly known any blacks in my life. It isn't an issue that I've thought about a lot. . . . I've got to learn a lot, and I've got to catch up fast."

President Kennedy knew that the black vote had been crucial in his election victory. He also knew that blacks had reason to be outraged; as a congressman and senator he had supported civil rights legislation. He was fond of quoting a set of statistics that he used in his first debate with Richard Nixon: "If a Negro baby is born . . . he has about one-half as much chance to get through high school as a white baby. He has one third as much chance to get through college as a white student. He has about a third as much chance to be a professional man, and about half as much chance to own a house. He has about four times as much chance that he'll be out of work in his life as the white baby. I think we can do better. I don't want the talents of any American to go to waste."

But how much help would James Meredith receive from the new president? Kennedy had deliberately echoed Abraham Lincoln in his inaugural address, and he could quote important statistics, but he had done little for black people that could compare with the actions of the "Great Emancipator."

The phone call to Coretta Scott King during the 1960 campaign represented a turning point in Kennedy's involvement with the black community. He was no grand spokesman on behalf of civil rights, but at a key moment his fundamental sense of decency overcame his instinctive political caution.

John Kennedy's actions as president were a constant balancing act. On the one hand, he was an idealist: He believed in pursuing a course devoted to high moral principles. On the other hand, he was a pragmatist: He believed that sometimes he had to be willing to compromise on principles to make sure that progress would be made. He often had genuine reform at heart, but on occasion abandoned principle in order to play the game of politics. This tactic helped him create change that would have been impossible if he had remained rigid in his beliefs. At other times he was too cautious, and he left those who believed in his causes feeling betrayed. No issue tested John Kennedy's balance between idealism and pragmatism more than did the question of civil rights.

Within hours of taking the oath of office, President Kennedy was exhibiting the sense of decency that endeared him to many in the black community. As he basked in the glow of the inaugural parade, he noticed that there were no blacks in the coast guard unit that saluted him. That night he called Treasury Secretary Dillon and demanded an explanation: Why weren't there any Negroes in that unit? The answer was simple: There were still no blacks in the Coast Guard Academy. Kennedy was angry. It would take more than a year, but in 1962 the Coast Guard Academy accepted its first black midshipman.

Kennedy made a genuine effort to include more blacks in the offices and institutions of the federal government. When he became president, most government agencies had few black employees. The president saw to it that the government undertook an intensive effort to recruit more African Americans for positions of responsibility.

Yet when it came to addressing the wider arena of American society, Kennedy moved more cautiously. He believed in the law, and he believed in a reasonable, moderate pursuit of justice. He distrusted spontaneous emotional action, and the intensity of the civil rights activists made him uneasy. As far as he was concerned, calm was the necessary condition for progress.

But black people felt that they had waited long enough. The past ten years had seen the rise of the civil rights movement, in which blacks and sympathetic whites worked together for justice and equality under the law. One of their first great victories came in 1955, when the black people of Montgomery, Alabama, refused to ride the city buses for a whole year until the city changed the law that required them to sit at the back and to give up their seat if a white person wanted it.

Now, in 1961, civil rights activists were still concerned about buses—this time about those that crossed state lines. The Supreme Court had declared that it was against federal law for interstate bus lines to have separate seating areas or waiting rooms for blacks and whites. In the South, however, where racism was still most obvious, the bus companies practiced business as usual: segregation of their white and black customers. Since the federal government was not enforcing its own law, civil rights workers decided to take matters into their own hands.

In May of 1961, a group of thirteen intrepid people set off on "Freedom

Rides'' into the Deep South. Their plan called for riders to sit in various combinations on buses. Some black riders sat in the front of the bus, while their white companions sat in the back. Some black and white Freedom Riders sat side by side. When the bus arrived at a depot, black riders would enter the terminal and try to use all the facilities, including those marked for whites only, while their white companions entered the areas marked "Colored." If they were assaulted, they did not respond in kind. They were committed to nonviolent resistance.

White racists met the Freedom Riders with bricks, knives, and iron pipes. They dragged the riders off buses, beat them viciously, and threatened to murder them. When the buses came into small towns, the local police would mysteriously disappear, and mobs would act without restraint. Outside Anniston, Alabama, a bus was ambushed and firebombed. The riders barely escaped with their lives. By insisting on their constitutional right to equality, the Freedom Riders showed the nation just how deeply racial prejudice was entrenched in the United States.

A Greyhound bus carrying Freedom Riders is set afire in Alabama. (spring 1961)

At the time of the Anniston episode, Jack Kennedy was preparing to go to Vienna and meet with Soviet Premier Nikita Khrushchev. The last thing he wanted was trouble at home. Racial violence made a lie of the United States's claims of democracy. When news of the incident reached him, the president phoned Harris Wofford, now his special assistant for civil rights. But instead of expressing outrage at the violent men who threw the stones and set the fires, Kennedy exploded at the Freedom Riders themselves.

"Stop them!" he shouted at Wofford, who was sympathetic to the riders' actions. "Get your friends off those buses."

Kennedy could not understand why some people felt that they had to risk their lives in order to bring about change. Eventually Robert Kennedy, appointed attorney general by his brother, did help protect the Freedom Riders through the Justice Department, but the civil rights activists felt betrayed.

In 1962, black leaders became more impatient. They were particularly angry because they felt that Kennedy had broken his promise. During the presidential campaign, Kennedy had pointed out that as president he would have the power to end segregation in government-funded housing by simply signing an executive order. A "stroke of the pen" would do the trick.

Yet more than a year after he had come into office, Kennedy had issued no such order. Thousands of civil rights activists decided that they needed to remind the president of his promise. They sent the White House thousands and thousands of ball-point pens! The pens piled up on Harris Wofford's desk, but the order remained unsigned.

Kennedy had reasons for moving slowly. Throughout the first eighteen months of his administration, political caution had ruled. The reality was that the Democrats had a narrow margin in Congress, and Kennedy was afraid that strong action on civil rights would offend Democratic senators from the South. The offended senators might well decide to block any of Kennedy's legislative efforts. Without those key Democratic votes, he worried that Congress would pass no major bills—including housing, welfare, and minimum-wage laws that would directly benefit all citizens, including blacks. The reasons may have been based on good politics, but they showed that the president was unwilling to take a risky leadership role on this question.

Events, however, were forcing his hand. Martin Luther King, Jr., continued to lead demonstrations, often for rights as basic as access to integrated bathrooms in department stores. Some whites struck back in anger, bombing black churches and beating civil rights workers who dared to challenge them. The situation was becoming increasingly volatile as pockets of the South became battlegrounds.

In the meantime, James Meredith patiently pursued his constitutional right to attend the University of Mississippi. By the fall of 1962, he had won a final injunction, and a federal court ordered the university to enroll him. That September, Meredith prepared to go to college.

Oxford, Mississippi, was boiling over. From all around the state, white people gathered to try to stop a black man from entering "Ole Miss." They were prepared to use bottles and rocks to stop Meredith from enrolling.

This time Jack Kennedy was ready, too. He had never fully understood the passion that spurred the Freedom Riders—he thought they were simply out to make trouble—but he saw Meredith's case differently. The man only wanted an education. Furthermore, the federal courts had ordered the University of Mississippi to admit Meredith. If nothing else, the president wanted to make sure that the people of Mississippi had some respect for the government of the United States.

Still, Kennedy tried to proceed as carefully as he could. He wanted to persuade the governor of Mississippi, Ross Barnett, that it was best for the state to give in. The last thing the president wanted was to bring in the army and force the university to admit the black man.

Barnett, however, did not see it that way. The governor knew that most white people in Mississippi did not want Meredith to enroll. He knew that the voters would be angry at *him* if he obeyed the federal government. Barnett knew that the federal government would eventually win, but he wanted to make it *seem* as though he was going to fight every inch of the way. If his position made Mississippians so angry that a mob formed and people were hurt . . . well, the governor could blame the violence on "the Kennedys."

Three times in late September 1962, members of the Justice Department accompanied Meredith when he tried to register for his classes. Three times Ross Barnett and other Mississippi politicians, backed by the state police, personally refused to obey the court order.

John Kennedy phoned Ross Barnett. He approached the governor as one politician to another, two men with a shared set of problems. "Go get him, Johnny boy," Robert Kennedy told his brother with a smile.

"Well, now, here's my problem," the president started. "I didn't put him in the university, but on the other hand, under the Constitution, I have to carry out that order. Now I'd like to get your help in doing that."

But Barnett argued that he had to obey his own state constitution, which permitted segregation. "I've taken an oath to do that," the governor answered, "and you *know* what our laws are with reference to . . ." He left the thought uncompleted, but the president knew that the governor would back the state's support of segregation rather than the federal government's demand for integration.

"What I would like to do," said Kennedy, "is to try to work this out in an amicable way. We don't want a lot of people getting hurt or killed down there."

It turned out that Barnett wanted the federal government to participate in a little play: Kennedy would send armed United States marshals to back up the court order. The governor would once again stand and block Meredith from registering. Then the marshals would draw their guns, and the governor and the state police would step aside. That way, Barnett would be able to say to the people of Mississippi, "See, they made me do it."

Always the politician, Kennedy gave his okay to this charade. But he was aware of the danger of his relaxed, casual conversations with Barnett. "You've been fighting a sofa pillow all week," he told Bobby Kennedy. Barnett may have seemed soft, but it was hard to budge him.

These arrangements, however, meant nothing on September 30, when James Meredith arrived in Oxford with the marshals. A crowd of 2,500 angry whites swarmed through the town, furious at Meredith and furious at the federal government. It was obvious that the marshals could not guarantee Meredith's safety, so they took him to a dormitory. There they waited as day gave way to evening. Shouts and curses rang through the gathering dark: "Kill the nigger-loving bastard." "Two-Four-One-Three, we hate Ken-ne-dy!"

At the White House, John Kennedy assumed, perhaps naively, that everything would go smoothly. At 10:00 P.M. (8:00 P.M. in Mississippi), he went on national television to tell the country calmly that "there is, in short, no reason why the books on this case cannot now be quickly closed in the manner directed by the court." He spoke quietly, forcefully, trying to give the impression that the federal government had everything under control.

In fact, nothing was under control. As soon as the president stepped away from the television lights, he rushed to the cabinet room, where he learned that things were falling apart in Oxford. The crowd was surging through the streets. Iron spikes were flying through the air. The first shotgun blasts echoed through town.

The men in the cabinet room were John Kennedy's closest advisors. First and foremost there was his younger brother Bobby, the attorney general, manning the phones and snapping orders to his men on the scene. Ted Sorensen, Kenny O'Donnell, and Larry O'Brien were there: young, serious men who had been with Kennedy since his days in Congress. Messages came in and went out through Evelyn Lincoln, the president's longtime personal secretary.

The atmosphere was like that of a wartime control center. To John Kennedy and his men, it was nearly as serious. If tensions escalated in Mississippi, hundreds of people might be killed or wounded, and the events might trigger violence all over the country.

Robert Kennedy learned that Meredith was trapped in his dormitory room. The mob was growing. The state police, whom Barnett had promised would keep order, had disappeared.

To the people in the White House cabinet room, the National Guard, with its nearest available troops stationed in Tennessee, was beginning to look like the only choice. "I'm going to see if I can get these troops started," Robert Kennedy said. "I don't think it's worth screwing around."

John Kennedy could only wait. It was frustrating, but in many situations all he could do was give his orders and hope that things took a turn for the better.

The president was noticeably impatient. He complained to Ted Sorensen about some bad press coverage, and he thought about calling the reporter to complain. He chatted about a current political thriller called *Seven Days in May*. "It's not any good," Kennedy complained. "The only character that came out at all was the general. The president was awfully vague." Kennedy even resorted to weak humor: "We have riots like this at Harvard just because some guy yells."

Soon afterward, Evelyn Lincoln took a message for the attorney general: "Would you tell him that a reporter for the *London Daily Sketch*, whose name is Paul Guihard, G-U-I-H-A-R-D, was killed in Oxford just now? His body was found with a bullet in the back, next to a women's dormitory." The crisis had claimed its first casualty.

The joking quickly stopped in the cabinet room. Now the pressing question was not whether troops should be used, but how fast they could be transported to Oxford to prevent further disaster. "They're storming where Meredith is," Robert Kennedy reported frantically.

From the midst of the chaos, Ross Barnett called to try to convince the president to back down. "Mr. President, please," Barnett wheedled. "Why can't you give an order up there to remove Meredith?"

The plea triggered a flash of anger in Kennedy. "How can I remove him, Governor, when there's a riot in the street, and he may step out of that building and something happen to him? I can't remove him under those conditions."

"But, but—" began Barnett.

Changing local and national laws was not enough to ensure equal rights for and equal treatment of all Americans.

"Let's get order up there," Kennedy snapped. "Then we can do something about Meredith."

But order was not restored until several thousand United States Army and National Guard troops arrived in Oxford in the early hours of the morning. In the cabinet room, there was an almost visible sigh of relief when Robert Kennedy was finally able to report that things seemed to be under control. "Yeah, but you see, we're going to be blamed for not doing enough," the attorney general commented sourly.

The night-long siege did not deter James Meredith, and the next day he formally enrolled as a student at the University of Mississippi. Over the next few weeks, thousands more troops arrived as threats of violence hovered over the campus.*

John Kennedy had withstood one of the greatest tests of his presidency. He had upheld the law, and at a crucial moment he had used federal troops to back up a man's right to an education.

The Mississippi crisis taught John Kennedy something that black Americans had known for a long time: Many whites would fight long and hard against equal rights. His dealings with Ross Barnett helped to convince the president that he could not trust the promises of some white politicians.

Kennedy also discovered that despite his brother's doubts, most Americans approved of the federal government's strong but restrained response. The crisis certainly helped remove some of the doubts that blacks had about the president's commitment to civil rights, but it did not convert him to a passionate backer of the movement. He still expected blacks—who had been entitled to equal rights under the U.S. Constitution for nearly 100 years—to be patient.

The president knew that this was just one small victory over the forces of racism. He was right when he muttered to no one in particular in the middle of the crisis, "It's going to be a long fall in Oxford."

*It was a long and difficult struggle, but in 1963 James Meredith became the first black graduate of the University of Mississippi. He had earlier earned credits from Jackson State College, a historically black institution.

During the May 1963 civil rights demonstrations in Birmingham, Alabama, police turned high-pressure fire hoses on the demonstrators.

Despite the victories at Mississippi and other schools, black Americans remained justifiably angry. In 1963, they marched in the streets of Birmingham, Alabama, because change was not coming quickly enough. Alongside the adults were children, some as young as seven and eight, who, like their parents, were willing to risk their lives for equality.

Martin Luther King, Jr., who led the Birmingham marches, urged his followers to practice strict nonviolence. Blacks were rightfully bitter at the injustices they suffered, but King preached that the civil rights movement must not meet bloodshed with bloodshed. He considered peaceful demonstrations the most powerful weapon against injustice. "Nonviolence is the summit of bravery," King said. "If we are arrested every day, if we are trampled over every day, don't ever let anyone pull you so low as to hate them. We must use the weapon of love."

The Birmingham police, however, met the marchers with dogs and high-pressure fire hoses. Jets of water drenched and pummeled the crowds of protestors. Photographs of the event exposed to the nation the brutality of the white racist establishment in the South.

Jack Kennedy, however, still could not understand why blacks took to the streets. When the president saw a photograph of a German shepherd with its teeth in the arm of one of the Birmingham demonstrators, he was "sickened." Yet when he met with advisors to decide how to meet the crisis, he blamed both the blacks and the whites for the violence. Although it was clear that whites were initiating the violence, the president did not place the blame squarely on the white leadership of the South. His reticence lost him some of the admiration of civil rights leaders that he had won during the "Ole Miss" crisis.

Part of the problem was that Kennedy was not comfortable with Dr. King. Both were men of shrewd political instinct and deep principle, but Kennedy was more of a pragmatist, King more of an idealist. Kennedy favored compromise on behalf of progress, whereas King believed that only through nonviolent confrontation could black Americans fully win the equality to which they were entitled. The styles of the two men clashed at every point.

King and Kennedy met several times during Kennedy's presidency, but their meetings were always forced and awkward. They never found a way of talking honestly with each other. King tended to lecture the president; Kennedy tended to avoid giving direct answers to the civil rights leader's pointed questions. They were the two most magnetic figures in the United States, yet they failed to establish a common ground. Kennedy's moderation, often a virtue, betrayed him in his relationship with King. It was the president, wary of the power of King's message, who ultimately sabotaged that relationship.

In 1963, FBI director J. Edgar Hoover convinced him that several of King's friends in the civil rights movement were Communist agents who were working to overthrow the government of the United States. The president gave the FBI permission to place a wiretap on King's telephone. Hoover gave no evidence to back up his charges, but John and Robert Kennedy were so worried about communism that they went along with this illegal invasion of King's privacy.

Indeed, when King visited the White House in June 1963, the president did not want to ask about the progress of the civil rights movement. As the two men strolled in the Rose Garden, Jack Kennedy put his hand on King's shoulder and told him that he had to "get rid of" the supposed Communist agents. Kennedy was concerned that suspicions of Communist influence might reflect badly on the government itself.

"If they shoot *you* down, they'll shoot *us* down, too," Kennedy warned.

King was flabbergasted and disappointed. Instead of giving his unqualified support to the civil rights cause, the president was spending his time worrying about petty political considerations. Any chance for the two men to truly know and understand each other was lost forever.

It is ironic that this lost chance with King came in the same month in which John Kennedy gave his most eloquent statement in support of equal rights for black Americans. Just one week earlier, the president had called out the National Guard to back up the admission of two black students to the University of Alabama. On the night of June 11, he went on national television to tell the American people that civil rights was a "moral cause," one "as old as the scriptures and as clear as the American Constitution."

"The fires of frustration and discord are burning in every city," John Kennedy told his audience. The moral crisis "cannot be quieted by token moves or talk. It is time to act in the Congress, in your state and local legislative bodies, and, above all, in all of our daily lives."

It was a speech that even Martin Luther King called a "masterpiece." With it, Kennedy proposed the boldest civil rights laws in a century. He introduced a bill that would protect blacks' right to vote, ban discrimination in restaurants and hotels, and give the attorney general real power to challenge seg-

President Kennedy with Martin Luther King, Jr., and other leaders of the 1963 March on Washington, the largest peaceful demonstration in the history of the United States.

regation in tax-supported public schools. "We're not turning back," Kennedy exclaimed. The new Civil Rights Act did not become law during Kennedy's lifetime, but the proposal showed that the man had grown during his presidency. He had come a long way since he told Harris Wofford to "get the Freedom Riders off the buses."

Yet Kennedy remained a politician to the end. Civil rights laws were a moral cause, but they were also a way of keeping black anger off the streets. By passing the laws, the president hoped that civil rights activism could be contained within government office buildings in Washington. Marches made him nervous.

Two hundred fifty thousand people gathered on August 28, 1963, for the March on Washington, the largest civil rights demonstration in United States history. Blacks and whites marched hand in hand through Washington, D.C., to celebrate civil rights victories and the new possibilities for equality in the United States. Together they raised their voices to let the government know much more needed to be done.

"I have a dream," Martin Luther King, Jr., told the throng. "I have a dream that my four little children will one day live in a nation where they will not be judged by the color of their skin, but by the content of their character."

Martin Luther King brought his speech to a rousing climax—"Free at last! Free at last! Thank God almighty, free at last!" A quarter million people joined their voices with his in a moment of triumph.

Jack Kennedy was in Washington, D.C., on the day that King told of his dream, but he was not with the speakers on the steps of the Lincoln Memorial. Fearful of violence, he had tried to persuade civil rights leaders not to hold the march, but he had reluctantly given it his support. On that August day, Kennedy and his advisors were waiting inside the White House, ready with proclamations that would bring in 19,000 troops waiting on alert in case the march got out of hand. No such action was necessary, as marchers celebrated with joy and dignity in the streets of the capital.

The president met with Dr. King and other civil rights leaders immediately after the march in a reception at the White House. The president gripped the minister's hand, offered his congratulations, and said, in tribute to one of King's most memorable lines, "I have a dream."

The president claps while Caroline and John, Jr., dance in the Oval Office.
(October 1962)

7

"One Hundred Thousand Welcomes"
(1961–1963)

**Earth's the right place for love:
I don't know where it's likely to go better.**

In an unusual move, John Kennedy had invited Robert Frost to read a poem at his inauguration. "He would remind us," the president commented, "that we are dealing with life, the hopes and fears of millions of people, and also tell us that our deep convictions must be the ultimate guide to our actions." Frost's participation marked "the beginning hour" of "a golden age of poetry and power"—an unprecedented celebration of the arts and humanities in American life.

Kennedy took a greater interest in promoting literature and the arts than did any president before or after him. He showed respect—even reverence—for creativity. The world of words, of language and literature, remained important to him throughout his life.

He never held himself up as a judge of taste and culture, but maintained the strongest conviction that poets and other artists touch the deepest wellspring of our national strength, for they have something to tell us about ourselves that might otherwise remain hidden. "I see little of more importance to the future of our country and our civilization than full recognition of the place of the artist." Always interested in defining and redefining the concept of courage, he saw one side of it in the work of the artist. "There are many kinds of courage," Kennedy said, "bravery under fire, courage to risk reputation and friendship and career for convictions which are deeply held. Perhaps the rarest courage of all—for the skill to pursue it is given to very few men— is the courage to wage a silent battle to illuminate the nature of man and the world in which he lives. . . ."

He understood the artistic process—the stern demands, the discipline, the hours a writer might spend over a single word or a composer over a single note—and he needed the nation to understand it. "I know that there is some feeling by Americans that the arts are developed in solitude, that they are developed by inspiration and by sudden fits of genius. But the fact of the matter is that success comes in music or in the arts like success comes in every other form of human endeavor—by hard work, by discipline, over a long period of time. Every musician here, every musician in the United States, every musician in the world plays after months and years of the most painstaking work, the kind of discipline which most people cannot endure."

One of the stories he liked to tell was about the mother who said to the school principal, "Don't teach my boy poetry. He is going to run for Congress." Clearly, for Kennedy, the world of politics and the world of poetry were much closer to each other than most people thought. "When power leads man towards arrogance," the president said, "poetry reminds him of his limitations. When power narrows the areas of man's concern, poetry reminds him of the richness and diversity of his existence. When power corrupts, poetry cleanses. For art establishes the basic human truth which must serve as the touchstone of our judgment."

The Kennedys brought the world of arts to the White House, and at the same time made several changes in the formal tone that had marked the stuffy Eisenhower years. They did away with tiring reception lines. For the first time in memory aperitifs and mixed drinks were served as guests entered, though the president himself rarely drank. Smoking was now permitted in the State Room. (Occasionally, the president would smoke a cigar in public.)

Somber affairs were replaced by lighthearted parties. People felt at ease. Warmth and good-natured fun characterized the new White House hospitality.

At a dinner honoring composer Igor Stravinsky, he and Leonard Bernstein, the conductor of the New York Philharmonic Symphony Orchestra, greeted each other in European style, embracing and kissing on both cheeks. Witnessing this from across the ballroom, Jack called out to the two men, "Hey, how about me?" Bernstein described the incident as "endearing and so insanely unpresidential."

On August 22, 1961, the first of a series of concerts—performed by young people for young people—was held on the south lawn of the White House. "I'm leaving my door open, so I can hear the whole concert," the president told the audience and musicians. He could not be with them during the performance, but he wanted them to know that he valued what they were doing.

Forty-nine Nobel Prize winners gathered at the White House on April 29, 1962. Kennedy held up his glass, tilted it in the direction of his guests, and said, "I think this is the most extraordinary collection of talent, of human knowledge, that has ever gathered together at the White House, with the possible exception of when Thomas Jefferson dined alone."

The performances were not totally smooth—the electricity blew out during a performance of *Brigadoon* by the New York City Center Ballet, and one of the young Metropolitan Opera Guild star performers wore a mink turban with three tall ostrich feathers that caught fire from candle flame in a wall sconce.

The president himself was given to small mistakes. During a luncheon, he addressed Prince Rainier of Monaco as "Prince Reindeer." Another time, thinking he was walking into the East Room, he escorted a visiting dignitary into the butler's pantry. "And this, Mr. President, is one of the historic rooms of the mansion, too," Kennedy remarked cheerfully when he realized his error. In the White House dining hall during a meal for young musicians, Kennedy received a handful of chocolate icing in a handshake from an eleven-year-old admirer. He licked his palm and grinned mischievously. "Mmmm good! I'll have to have a piece of that, too!"

The president was a proud and doting father, taking enormous pride in his children's achievements, big or small: Caroline's growing skill as a horseback rider, her affinity for books and words, her strong swimming; and John, Jr.'s, first words and first steps.

With an office at home, Kennedy had easy access to the children. Caroline and ten other children attended nursery school in the White House. During recess they would come running when they heard the president clap twice—the signal that he was free and would love to see them. On other occasions, Caroline and her English nanny, Maud Shaw, watched official festivities through the banister railings.

He loved playing with the children, whether it was pretending that he and John, Jr., were helicopter pilots in the hangar at Camp David or swimming with Caroline in the White House pool. For the president, playing with his children was a relief from the heavy pressures of the job.

Once, a White House staff member glimpsed the president crawling after the children on all fours; he looked away when he saw the president bump his head on a table. Jack Kennedy lamented that he could not lift the children because of his back, and he often encouraged his friends to throw them up in the air. When Caroline walked into a press conference wearing her mother's high-heeled shoes, the president chuckled, and when John, Jr., interrupted a speech being recorded in the Executive Office, the president maintained his poise and good nature.

Kennedy enjoyed telling his children stories. One day on his boat, the *Honey Fitz*, with Franklin Delano Roosevelt, Jr., sitting beside him, he invented a story for Caroline about a whale. Roosevelt's legs were crossed, his shoes were off, and on his feet was a dirty pair of sweat socks. In the story the whale most loved to eat dirty old sweat socks. The president reached over, took off one of Roosevelt's socks, and threw it overboard. With rapt attention Caroline watched the sock disappear, thinking that the whale had devoured it; then the president reached over and took off the other sock. Caroline watched transfixed as that sock, too, was lost beneath the surface of the water.

The children were always accompanied by three Secret Service men who

A quiet moment with his daughter, Caroline. (August 1963)

became like uncles to them. In April of 1961, a plot to kidnap Caroline was revealed. The Secret Service code-named everyone in the first family. Caroline was Lyric; John, Jr., Lark; the president, Lancer; and the First Lady, Lace. The code names enabled the Secret Service to talk about the family without outsiders knowing whom they were talking about.

Despite his allergy to dogs, Kennedy loved them, and at one point the family had nine, including an Irish wolfhound, a Welsh terrier, and a cocker spaniel. In addition, they had a yellow canary, a gray cat, two hamsters that often escaped from their cage, several ducks, and two ponies—Leprechaun and Macaroni. Some evenings, President and Mrs. Kennedy would take two of the dogs for a walk outside the White House grounds. Worried Secret Service men followed.

In the eyes of the nation and the world, the president and the First Lady were phenomena. Jack used an old-fashioned rocking chair to ease the strain on his back, and rocking chairs became popular again. Mannequins with a striking similarity to Jackie were displayed in store windows everywhere. Models resembling the First Lady appeared in fashion shows. A movie magazine featured Jackie with actress Elizabeth Taylor on the cover highlighting "America's two queens." Every dress she wore, every breath she took, became big news. The "Jackie look" was the rage. The First Lady was horrified and embittered by what she saw. "I feel as if I've been turned into a piece of public property."

A song-and-dance ensemble on a popular television show responded cheerfully to the president's charge to the nation to join in his program for physical fitness:

> Dear President Kennedy,
> You said we were a nation of softies
> You said we were not physically fit.
> Dear JFK, the very next day, we determined to do our bit. . . .
> Everybody's doin' it, doin' it, doin' it,
> Inhale, exhale, straighten and bend. . . .

Entertainer Vaughn Meader imitated the president in voice and dress and even began to cut his hair like the president's. He did a persuasive imitation of Jack Kennedy and made a humorous record album that sold thousands of copies.

One reporter was interested in Kennedy's reaction to the heavy dose of teasing that comedians were dishing out. "Mr. President, it's been a long time since a president and his family have been subjected to such a heavy barrage of teasing and fun-poking and satire. There have been books like *Backstairs at the White House*, cartoon books with clever sayings, photo albums with balloons and the rest, and now a smash hit record. Can you tell us whether you read and listen to these things and whether they produce annoyment or enjoyment?"

The president responded, "Annoyment? No. Yes, I have read them and listened to them and actually I listened to Mr. Meader's record, but I thought it sounded more like Teddy than it did me—so he's annoyed."

The bustling family activity and festive affairs of state would eventually lead many to think of the White House as a modern-day Camelot, echoing Jack's love of King Arthur and the popularity of the Lerner and Loewe musical. In the popular imagination the Kennedys were as close to royalty as the United States had ever been, and the White House was the seat of Kennedy's court.

The media exploitation of the Kennedys, the family tumult, the light-hearted parties took place amid ongoing national and world problems. As Kennedy said, "In eleven weeks I went from senator to president, and in that short space of time I inherited Laos, Cuba, Berlin, the nuclear threat, and all the rest." The job of the presidency was far harder than he thought it would be, the burdens far heavier.

In the White House no day was quite like the one before, and every day was hectic. "When you are around here you have to eat fast, read fast, think fast, and sleep fast, or else you won't get anything done," the president commented. Within minutes after President Kennedy opened his eyes at about 7:45 A.M., he was practically blanketed in newsprint. In his nightshirt and wearing his horn-rimmed glasses, he scanned several morning newspapers. His eyes coursed down the columns on the page at about twelve hundred words a minute—at least three times faster than average reading speed. Often, he would call his advisors to see if they had seen a particular news item, and he clipped articles and asked aides to verify them. The president liked to know details, and he knew how to ask direct questions that produced direct answers. In self-defense his aides became faithful newspaper readers.

Mornings, his children visited him, tumbling around on the bed in the midst of the newspapers, and then scrambled onto the floor to watch television cartoons. The president continued reading through the children's clatter and the noise of the television.

There was no freedom he valued more deeply than freedom of the press. He viewed journalism, in *Washington Post* editor Benjamin C. Bradlee's words, as "the first rough draft of history." No one was more aware of the power of the press than the president.

In Hyannis Port, the president takes his daughter and her cousins for a ride in a golf cart. (summer 1963)

Kennedy was at ease with journalists, counting some, such as Bradlee, among his closest friends. He was delighted when an article about him was favorable, furious when it was unfavorable. Although he was honest in private about his own shortcomings, he was sensitive to criticism. One reporter complained: "He wants us as a cheering squad." At the outset of his administration he saw the press as an extension of the Oval Office. With the media on his side, the information he wanted the nation to know would be publicized.

John Fitzgerald Kennedy was the first president to allow his press conferences to be broadcast live on radio and television. In previous administrations, questions had to be submitted to the chief executive in advance, but Kennedy faced hundreds of reporters without knowing precisely what they would ask. "It's like preparing for a final exam twice a month," he commented. When he went into the conference, he was edgy and worried about whether he was adequately prepared, sometimes feeling like a lamb about to be thrown to the lions. But he loved watching the rebroadcast and was inevitably pleased with what he saw, laughing aloud at some of his own puns. When one reporter asked, "How is your aching back?" the president responded, "It depends on the weather, political or otherwise."

Once he was asked, "I wonder if you could tell us if you had to do it all over again, would you work for the presidency and whether you can recommend the job to others?" The president replied, "Well, the answer to the first is yes and the second is no. I don't recommend it, at least for a while."

Sixty-five million people watched his first press conference, held on February 1, 1961. In all, he held sixty-four televised press conferences. Each began with the president's announcements and ended with the words of the senior correspondent, "Thank you, Mr. President."

Jackie Kennedy's feelings about the press were far less friendly. Even when her press secretary arranged formal meetings with journalists, she refused to honor the commitment. She was also far more protective of the children than her husband was, fighting a battle to preserve their privacy, to protect them from further exploitation by the press. When one correspondent asked her what she fed her new German shepherd pup, she retorted, "Reporters."

In order to ease his grinding back pain, the president swam twice daily in the heated White House pool. Usually, Dave Powers swam with him, and the two friends talked about sports events or reminisced about the president's political beginnings in the 1946 congressional campaign and the fateful day when Jack knocked on Powers's door. Although not a political advisor, he served as special assistant to the president. He entertained his boss with campaign statistics, Irish jokes and stories, and baseball lore. The children knew Dave better than any man besides their father.

The president trusted him. No matter how worried or how discouraged he felt, Dave Powers could make him feel better. Dave was often humorously referred to as the "court jester" or "John's other wife."

Even after he became president, John Kennedy maintained his friendships with those who had meant much to him in earlier times, forming a "band of brothers." A composite portrait of his loyal fellowship revealed people in splendid variety—the athlete, the jester, the banker, the statesman, the scribe, the artist, the merchant—each with a feeling for the president that went beyond simple affection.*

His friends have identified many personal characteristics: his disarming humor, his vitality, his charm. "He could say 'Pass the salt,' and I was deeply touched," remembered composer Leonard Bernstein. He had a fundamental decency that prevented him from hating people. "He was a most forgiving man," said his close friend Ben Bradlee. "I disliked people that *he* should have disliked," Lem Billings recalled.

Lem Billings more or less inhabited a third-floor White House guest room, even keeping his clothes there. No matter how many years passed, Jack and

---

*Kennedy's close friends included Torbert Macdonald (his Harvard roommate, swim-team companion, and later a congressman); Dave Powers (known for his wit); James Reed (a war buddy who became assistant secretary of the treasury); Lord Harlech (a friend from the time Jack spent as a young man in England, later British ambassador to the United States); Benjamin Bradlee (bureau chief of *Newsweek*); William Walton (an artist and later chairman of the Fine Arts Commission); and Paul "Red" Fay (a buddy from PT training-school days, who later went into business in San Francisco).

John, Jr., rocks in a spare rocking chair. (October 1963)

Lem remained the lively Choate roommates of old, trying the patience of their elders and sharing memories. From the time they were at boarding school and Jack took him home, Lem was a member of the family, another brother. In defining who they were to each other, the word *friendship* seems inadequate. Jack's sister Eunice observed: "President Kennedy was a completely liberated man when he was with Lem." He appreciated Lem's devotion, and returned it. Although he could not assume the burdens of the presidency, there is little question that Lem Billings would have given his life for Kennedy.

His closest friends and advisors were men; his secretary, Evelyn Lincoln, and Jacqueline Kennedy were the only two women who consistently participated in the president's political life. The Kennedy team was also, with a handful of exceptions, white, and the president drew heavily on graduates of Harvard University and other Ivy League schools.

The presidency, despite the surrounding crowd, was lonelier than Kennedy had ever foreseen—far harder, far more treacherous than any campaign, far more dangerous and more frustrating than his father had led him to believe or he himself could have imagined. In a sense, fate had thrown him into a position of political power. He could not refuse the position, although he was not sure he was capable of mastering it. "My father always knew that if anything happened to Joe I would run," Kennedy said, "and that if anything happened to me, Bobby would run, and that if anything happened to Bobby, Teddy would run."

Although he kept up appearances as a devoted family man, Jack Kennedy, like his father, pursued relationships with many women. He had dated widely before he married Jacqueline Bouvier, and he continued a long and intricate series of affairs throughout his presidency. He seemed obsessed by the idea of conquest. Members of the press were sometimes aware of the president's activities, but they kept details out of the papers. Although the true nature and number of John Kennedy's affairs will never be known, some people have connected him with Judith Campbell Exner (who had ties with the Mafia), abstract painter Mary Pinchot (whom Jack had known from his Choate days), and Marilyn Monroe (the most spectacular movie star of the time).

Some evenings, when Jackie and the children took a vacation, the president and Dave Powers were alone after a long, rough day. They would fend for themselves in the White House kitchen, heating the fish chowder left by the cook and eating at the kitchen table. On warm days they would leave the dishes in the sink and go to the Truman balcony, where Jack did his home-work, reading reports in preparation for meetings the following day. He would listen to music, talk about old times, call Jackie on the phone. He once quipped to Dave: "This is the best White House I ever lived in." At about 11 P.M. the two friends would head toward the sleeping quarters and, on their knees be-side the president's bed, say their prayers together. Then Jack would stretch out in bed and, as Dave turned to leave, would say, "Good night, pal, will you please put out the light?" To his friends this boyish trust was one of his most endearing qualities.

When he bid farewell to the crowds in Galway on his 1963 visit to Ireland, he told the people that if they came to the United States, they should stop in Washington and tell the White House gatekeepers that they were from Gal-way; "and when you do, it will be 'Céad Míle Fáilte,' which means 'One

Relaxing aboard the *Honey Fitz*. (August 1963)

hundred thousand welcomes.' " People delighted in this magnanimity of spirit, this capacity to befriend and to extend hospitality to the stranger.

In April 1963, two months before the president's trip to Ireland, the White House announced that the First Lady was expecting a baby. Because of her history of difficult pregnancies, Jackie curtailed all official duties. The new baby would be the first infant to take up residence in the White House in sixty-three years. The birth was expected in September, but in early August, a helicopter rushed Jackie from her seclusion in Hyannis Port to the nearby military hospital at Otis Air Force Base. She gave birth to a four-pound-ten-and-one-half-ounce baby boy, delivered five and one-half weeks early by cesarean section. He was baptized Patrick Bouvier Kennedy after the president's great-grandfather and Jackie's father. Patrick suffered respiratory problems and lived only thirty-nine hours. "He put up quite a fight," the president said, deeply shaken and weeping. "He was a beautiful baby."

The funeral service was led by the priest who had married the Kennedys, Cardinal Cushing of Boston, and attended by immediate family members. The president was the last to leave. Brokenhearted, he placed his arms around the tiny casket and had to be coaxed away from it by Cushing, who whispered, "Come on, Jack. Let's go. God is good."

Despite the tribulations of his personal life and his office, John F. Kennedy delighted in the presidency. Only rarely did he express dismay or frustration about the job. He viewed the office as "the vital center of action," and radiating from this center were far-reaching concerns, both domestic and foreign. More than any other person, he knew the promise of his administration; few could know the perils.

"There is always inequity in life," said Kennedy. "Some men are killed in a war, and some are wounded, and some men never leave the country . . . it's very hard in military or in personal life to assure complete equality. Life is unfair. Some people are sick and others are well." He was especially attracted to a line in one of Robert Frost's poems, "I have been one acquainted with the night."

On a crisp Saturday in October of 1963, the president traveled to Amherst College in Massachusetts to take part in a ceremony honoring Frost, who had died in late January of that year. "A nation reveals itself not only by the men it produces but by the men it honors—the men it remembers," he told the audience. Kennedy spoke eloquently of Frost's contribution to America. "We must never forget that art is not a form of propaganda. It is a form of truth." The president sketched a vision of a nation where artistic excellence and the national purpose reinforced each other.

> I look forward to a great future for America, a future in which our country will match its military strength with our moral restraint, its wealth with our wisdom, its power with our purpose.
>
> I look forward to an America which will not be afraid of grace and beauty, which will protect the beauty of our natural environment, which will preserve the great old American houses and squares and parks of our national past, and which will build handsome and balanced cities for our future.
>
> I look forward to an America which will reward achievement in the arts as we reward achievement in business or statecraft. . . .
>
> I look forward to an America which commands respect throughout the world not only for its strength but for its civilization as well. And I look forward to a world which will be safe not only for democracy and diversity but also for personal distinction.

John Kennedy believed that the forces that bring people together are greater than those that divide them, and that hope is more powerful than despair. That faith was sorely tested by events around the world during his administration.

The Cold War was only one of the problems that faced Kennedy during his presidency. (May 1960)

8

The President and the World
(1961–1963)

And life is too much like a pathless wood

When John Kennedy took office in 1961, many people saw the world as a battleground. On one side stood the United States and its western allies, committed in principle to democracy and free enterprise. On the other side stood the Soviet Union and the Communist bloc, regarded in the United States as brutal and totalitarian. Outside the western and the eastern alliances stood the less-developed and poorer nations in Asia, Africa, and South and Central America. Many Americans saw world affairs as a contest between West and East for the souls of those developing nations.

It was, in many ways, a frightening view of the world. In World War II, fighting on a scale hitherto unknown had claimed millions of lives. Now, fifteen years later, the world had divided into opposing camps. Distrust and fear were in the air. The United States and the Soviet Union continued to build thousands of nuclear warheads, and each believed that the other was prepared to use them. (Only the United States, at Hiroshima and Nagasaki, had actually done so, at the end of World War II.) Trivial misunderstandings threatened to ignite nuclear war.

John Kennedy, too, was steeped in this fearful, threatening view of world affairs. The thrill of competition drilled into him at the family dinner table extended to the international arena. When his father was ambassador to Great Britain, Jack had watched that nation underestimate the threat of Nazism in the 1930s. He wrote *Why England Slept* to warn Americans against the prospect of taking the German threat lightly. Although Jack was not as rabid an anticommunist as his father, as a senator he had carefully avoided taking a strong stand against the "red-baiting" of Senator Joseph McCarthy.

Later, as president, Kennedy accepted without hesitation the national consensus that the United States should be the greatest, most powerful nation in the world. To do so required effort and sacrifice, the kind of commitment Kennedy asked of the American people in his inaugural address. It also led to the belief that the United States should direct world affairs and that Americans should commit themselves to possible conflict with nations that held differing ideas. It was a view primed for confrontation. It was a spirit that led many to believe that the United States had the right, even the obligation, to tinker in the internal affairs of other nations, while deeply resenting the notion that others might interfere in its own domestic concerns.

When Kennedy took office, the United States seemed to be losing ground in world affairs. The Russians were tightening their hold on the countries of Eastern Europe, particularly East Germany. In Southeast Asia, a Communist-led guerrilla movement was challenging the fragile government that the French had set up in Vietnam. In the island nation of Cuba, ninety miles from Florida, an avowed Marxist, Fidel Castro, had come to power in 1959, when a corrupt U.S.-backed government was overthrown. Most embarrassing of all, the Russians had scored a massive public relations and scientific victory by launching the world's first spacecraft, *Sputnik I*, in 1957.

Seeking to seize the initiative, Kennedy drew on his strength—his ability to generate enthusiasm when faced with a challenge. During the campaign, Kennedy had endorsed the idea of a Peace Corps, in which Americans would volunteer to help people in the world's poorer nations. The idea had been trumpeted principally by his old Democratic rival, Senator Hubert Humphrey. Kennedy's mention of the idea was typically cautious: He tried it out at a rally at the University of Michigan at two in the morning. A group of the students inspired by his call tracked him down at a later campaign stop in Ohio. There they presented him with a petition containing the names of several hundred volunteers. After that, the idea became a central part of Kennedy's plans for the White House.

Jack Kennedy signed the executive order that established the Peace Corps in March of 1961. In doing so, he sounded a familiar theme: the necessity of sacrifice, and its rewards. The program was headed by his brother-in-law, Sargent Shriver. Kennedy also revived a program called Food for Peace, through which food worth billions of dollars was shipped overseas. He launched the Alliance for Progress, an effort to build economic bridges between the United States and the countries of Central and South America.

To Kennedy, these programs were examples of the tremendous good that the United States could achieve. Food for Peace and the Peace Corps brought much-needed supplies, expertise, and goodwill to millions of people around the world, though they scarcely affected the underlying problems of the world economy. The administration regarded humanitarian programs as weapons in the confrontation between democracy and communism: American ideas and know how could solve any problem. Kennedy hoped that the nations of the world could eventually be persuaded to see that the United States's version of democracy was the best of all possible governments.

Kennedy suffered a bitter initiation into the realms of military planning and operations. Shortly after his election, military officials from the Eisenhower administration briefed him on plans to overthrow Fidel Castro's government in Cuba. The plans reflected those leaders' uneasiness about the presence of a Communist country so close to the American coastline. The defense establishment under Eisenhower decided to use the best available resource: men who hated Castro and who had fled from Cuba after his revolution against the Batista dictatorship. They devised a plan to use American

Fidel Castro, premier of Cuba and frequent nemesis of the Kennedy administration. (c. 1960)

military experts to train the exiles in secret and prepare them for an armed assault on Cuba. They did not have enough manpower to mount a major attack, but the military strategists naively believed that thousands of people in Cuba would spontaneously revolt against Castro once they learned of the invasion.

In a series of meetings in February and March of 1961, Kennedy made a crucial mistake: He kept several of his most trusted advisors out of key meetings that he held with representatives of the military establishment and the Central Intelligence Agency (CIA). The operation was planned under a veil of secrecy that excluded many of the president's confidants. The generals and the CIA advisors told him that the invasion of Cuba would be a success, that American troops need not be involved, that the Castro regime would tumble under the slightest pressure.

The president was tempted. Toppling Castro would be a forceful beginning for his administration and would remove an irritating thorn in America's side. Toward the end of the decision-making process, he finally brought in advisors such as Robert Kennedy and Ted Sorensen. By that time, however, the plan was already in place. These men showed their loyalty to Jack Kennedy by declining to question a decision that the president had already made.

On April 17, 1961, a ragtag group of 1,500 Cuban exiles landed at the Bay of Pigs, on the southern coast of Cuba. Almost immediately their assault was met by well-armed Cuban divisions, and the invasion was quickly in trouble. The Cuban government rounded up thousands of people in Havana, ending any hope of an internal uprising. Worse still, the military experts had assured Kennedy that if the invasion failed, the invaders could take to the hills and begin a guerrilla war; they had failed to take into account the miles of marshland surrounding the Bay of Pigs. The invasion force was trapped, and nearly all were captured. It was a grim moment for the president, but he resisted the temptation to try to save the situation by openly using United States military forces.

Quite properly, Kennedy publicly accepted full responsibility for the fiasco, but he did not apologize for the reasons behind it. It remained to him a noble plan, stupidly executed. He held fast to his rigid conviction that the United States should try to impose its own beliefs on other nations. "The complacent, the self-indulgent, the soft societies are about to be swept away with the debris of history," he told a group of newspaper editors in explaining the incident. "Only the strong, only the industrious, only the determined, only the courageous, only the visionary who determine the real nature of our struggle can possibly survive." Kennedy continued to underestimate the toughness of Cuba and other developing countries, just as he overestimated the power of the United States to shape the courses of other nations.

Kennedy savored the image of the isolated leader bearing the burden of state. "There's a saying that victory has a hundred fathers but defeat is an orphan," he said after the event. By cultivating this idea, Kennedy was able to turn the whole mess into a public relations victory, at least as far as many people in the United States were concerned. When he accepted the blame, he made a misguided act seem like an act of courage. He cast himself as the lonely man of principle bravely swallowing the bitter pill of failure. Kennedy was aware of the gap between his actual performance and the national perception of it. One month after the Bay of Pigs, a public opinion poll showed that eighty-two percent of the American people approved of his performance in office. "It's like Eisenhower," the president said, laughing. "The worse I do the more popular I get."

Never again would the president keep his closest advisors so removed from the making of crucial decisions. Robert Kennedy, whose responsibilities as attorney general were officially concerned with domestic matters, was increasingly brought into discussions of foreign affairs. "I should have had Bobby in on this from the start," Jack confessed in May. Kennedy did not, however, retreat from public boldness in the aftermath of failure. Just seven weeks later, he outlined a "freedom doctrine," in which he reiterated his belief that developing nations were the battleground between democracy and communism.

In the first weeks of his presidency, Kennedy had been cautious about the space program, unwilling to commit himself to the massive expenditures required for each project. But later in the spring, struggling to keep his administration's momentum, Kennedy recognized that the Soviets would have to be met on their own ground. They had put the first man into space. The United States was not to be outdone. Toward the end of May he spoke before Congress and made a pledge: "I believe that this nation should commit itself to achieving the goal, before this decade is out, of landing a man on the moon and returning him safely to earth."

Yet the speech that promised the United States the moon was still couched in the timidity that produced the Bay of Pigs. Kennedy had already requested a massive military arms buildup, spending more on new weapons systems than at any time in the country's history. Now he also asked Congress to develop, for the first time, an extensive civil defense plan designed to save lives in the event of a nuclear war. World events convinced the president that it was a real possibility. Military studies projected that 70 million unprotected Americans (out of a population of 179 million) would be killed in an all-out war, but that only 50 million would be killed if the United States had a complete network of fallout shelters. Kennedy considered nuclear attack such a real possibility that he was willing to build a network of expensive underground bunkers to save 20 million lives.

Tensions continued to rise in June of 1961, when Kennedy met with Soviet Premier Nikita Khrushchev in Vienna, Austria. Although they chatted light-heartedly at times, the leaders of the two superpowers left Vienna without agreeing to resolve or end conflicts in any of the world's hot spots: Southeast Asia, Europe, Central America. As the leaders said good-bye, Kennedy gave Khrushchev his grim assessment of the lack of accord: "It will be a cold winter," he told the premier.

Long before winter, Kennedy's prediction came true. The German city of Berlin had been surrounded on all sides by East German territory since World War II. In August, the Soviet Union began to construct a wall creating the cities of East and West Berlin, effectively sealing off West Berlin. Kennedy decided that as long as West Berlin was not itself invaded, he would not challenge the Soviets, and the Wall became a concrete symbol of the Iron Curtain between Western and Eastern Europe. In September, the Soviet Union resumed testing nuclear weapons, and Kennedy announced that the United States would follow suit.

While the spirit of Camelot reigned in the White House, while the youthful president and his wife invited artists and entertainers to invigorate the cultural life of the nation's capital, while the Kennedy style graced the covers of fashion magazines, Jack Kennedy presided over a nation where children were taught to protect themselves by cowering under their desks in air raid drills—even as it was obvious that a desk would provide no protection from the terrifying force and deadly radiation of a nuclear explosion.

Nikita Khrushchev and John Kennedy at their only summit meeting. (Vienna, 1961)

On the morning of October 16, 1962, John Kennedy was eating breakfast when he was interrupted by his National Security Advisor, McGeorge Bundy. Bundy presented the president with a sheaf of photographs that showed conclusively that the Soviet Union was installing missiles in Cuba. The weapons were capable of striking anywhere on the East Coast of the United States. It was clear that the construction of the missile sites was not yet complete, but it might be only a few days before the silos would be ready to house nuclear warheads. There was no time to lose. Once the weapons were in place and on target, the United States would face a very real threat. There was no time to consult with allies, no time to work through the formalities of the United Nations. The crisis demanded a response.

Kennedy had learned a lesson from the Bay of Pigs. The Executive Committee (later dubbed the ExComm) that met to discuss this crisis included not only the top military advisors, but Robert Kennedy and several of the key aides who had been excluded from the earlier episode. ExComm meetings were free-floating, wide-ranging affairs. Kennedy was present, but he let others do most of the talking. He asked his usual clear, incisive questions but refused, at first, to commit himself as he sifted through the opinions voiced by his top advisors.

There was agreement that swift action was essential. But what? In the first meetings, discussion centered on an immediate military response—an attack by air or by sea. It was the only way, some advisors argued, that the message would be absolutely clear: The weapons must not be installed.

Kennedy first leaned toward a military response. But as the week wore on, the dangers of a quick strike at the missile site became more obvious. What if the Russian deployment was some sort of a bluff designed to provoke the United States into taking the first steps toward war? The president was not sure what the Soviets had in mind. Why didn't photographs reveal nuclear-warhead storage sites? Where were the troops that presumably should have been on hand to protect the sites?

"Well, it's a goddamn mystery to me," Kennedy said as the ExComm pondered the photographs. "I don't know enough about the Soviet Union, but if anybody can tell me any other time since the Berlin blockade where the Russians have given us so clear provocation, I don't know when it's been."

Robert McNamara, the Secretary of Defense, proposed a more moderate response. Rather than launch an air strike, the United States should undertake a naval blockade to stop the steady stream of Soviet ships that were taking military supplies to Cuba. It was an attractive option to Kennedy, a middle course between immediate military action and simply letting the Russians install the weapons. It would send a strong signal but would not allow the Soviets to claim that the United States had initiated a war.

The plan was kept secret until Monday, October 22. Kennedy did his best to maintain an appearance of public calm. At four that afternoon, he kept an appointment with the prime minister of Uganda and chatted about the state of affairs in Africa. Then, at seven that evening, he went on national television to inform the American people of the gravest threat to the national security since Pearl Harbor.

"Our goal," the president said, "is not the victory of might, but the vindication of right—not peace at the expense of freedom, but both peace *and* freedom, here in this hemisphere, and, we hope, around the world." United States Navy ships and Air Force planes were immediately dispatched to the Caribbean Sea to interrupt Soviet shipping. Among the warships sent by the navy was the destroyer *Joseph P. Kennedy, Jr.*

Yet peace was by no means assured. Over the weekend, the president had called Jackie and the children back from Glen Ora, Virginia, so that the family could be together in the emergency. Plans were made for the protection of the administration's top officials if the Soviets decided to respond with a nuclear attack on Washington, D.C. The blockade was a moderate response, but the Soviets had taken a bold and perilous step when they attempted to establish missile bases in Cuba, and no one was sure what they would do next.

For the next several days, the United States hovered on the brink of war. Khrushchev sent an angry letter. Russian warships continued on their course across the Atlantic. Photographs showed a flurry of activity at the missile sites. The U.S. military was put on alert, troops massed in Florida, and Kennedy threatened an invasion of Cuba.

But under the pressure, the Soviets backed down. Rather than challenge the blockade, the warships turned around and headed back to Europe. Khrushchev, while claiming that the weapons were there to defend Cuba from United States aggression, agreed to dismantle them. Kennedy and the ExComm breathed a collective sigh of relief. "We're eyeball to eyeball, and I think the other fellow just blinked," quipped Secretary of State Dean Rusk.

Children greet the president on his 1962 tour of South America.

Kennedy refused to gloat, and he refused to let those around him trumpet the Soviet retreat as a major victory for his administration. He was determined not to humiliate Khrushchev and provoke the Soviet premier further. He had acted prudently; he had avoided disaster; he wanted the nation to move on.

After the Bay of Pigs invasion, Kennedy had felt alone. After the Cuban

Missile Crisis, he was thankful for the men who shared that threat with him. To show his appreciation, he designed and ordered thirty-four silver calendars from Tiffany and Co., the famous New York jewelry firm. The mementos depicted the month of October 1962, with the thirteen days from October 16 to October 28 engraved more deeply than the other dates. He sent the calendars to ExComm members and to others who helped him.

In the aftermath of the Cuban Missile Crisis, Kennedy's international reputation, already considerable, became even greater. Throughout his presidency, Kennedy had fascinated foreigners. His foreign tours were marked by enthusiastic crowds who patiently put up with his botched attempts to speak to them in their own languages. The president's greatest triumph came on his trip in June 1963 to the embattled city of West Berlin. Thousands of Germans lined the streets to catch a glimpse of the motorcade, and thousands more packed into Rudolf Wilde Platz to hear Kennedy praise Berlin as the great holdout in the fight against communism. The Berlin Wall, said the president, demonstrated the failure of communism because it showed that force was the only way to prevent people from deserting Communist East Germany. "All free men," concluded Kennedy, "wherever they may live, are citizens of Berlin, and therefore, as a free man, I take pride in the words '*Ich bin ein Berliner.*'"

(The phrase, one of the most famous of John Kennedy's remarks, drew a few affectionate laughs from the crowd because his German was not quite correct. The president had meant to say, "*Ich bin Berliner,*" that is, "I am a citizen of Berlin." Instead, he proudly told his audience, "*Ich bin ein Berliner*"—"I am a jelly doughnut.")

Despite the drama of the Cuban Missile Crisis, despite the tough rhetoric of Berlin, the Kennedy administration was inching toward progress in its relationship with the Soviet Union. Although both countries had resumed testing nuclear weapons during Kennedy's presidency, both were looking for a way to stop. Testing escalated the arms race, and it encouraged both countries to develop new weapons too quickly. It was also dangerous in itself, since every above-ground explosion released deadly atmospheric radiation.

"Ich bin ein Berliner." John Kennedy delivers his famous speech in West Berlin. (June 1963)

In the early 1960s, scientists were beginning to understand the peril of nuclear fallout: that it would remain dangerous for hundreds, perhaps thousands, of years. One afternoon, Kennedy stood by the window in the Oval Office watching a steady downpour soak the capital. He asked his science advisor, Jerome Wiesner, how nuclear fallout reached the earth.

"It comes down in rain," Wiesner replied.

"You mean there might be radioactive contamination in that rain out there right now?" He stared pensively out the window.

In August 1963, the United States and the Soviet Union signed the Limited Nuclear Test Ban Treaty, the first arms-control agreement in the nuclear age. The superpowers agreed to stop all above-ground testing, although underground explosions would still be permitted. It was not a sweeping measure. The United States and the Soviet Union continued to build nuclear weapons—enough to destroy the earth several times over. But the ban represented a dramatic achievement for two nations that had been "eyeball to eyeball" over Cuba less than a year before. The treaty was one of John Kennedy's most tangible political triumphs, a huge step forward from the fearful anticommunism of the era.

In the tiny country of South Vietnam, halfway around the globe, the United States was taking another first step. The Kennedy administration, following a course begun under President Eisenhower, had been sending increasing numbers of military advisors to help shore up the government of President Ngo Dinh Diem. Diem presided over a corrupt government that had originally been established by the United States. He was under increasing pressure from discontented people in South Vietnam and from the Communist government of North Vietnam. As in Cuba, the United States naively believed that the people of Vietnam would seize any opportunity to resist the advance of communism.

In 1963, however, events in Vietnam were acquiring an intensity that Kennedy and his men were simply unable to understand. The chief of the secret police, Diem's brother, Ngo Dinh Nhu, ordered a vicious attack on the country's Buddhist pagodas. In protest, a Buddhist monk burned himself alive in a public square. Nhu's wife ordered that the sacred fish in a Buddhist shrine be poisoned. These and other conflicts eventually led, on November 2, 1963, to a military coup that toppled Diem's government; Diem and Nhu were both assassinated.

The revolt threw United States plans in Vietnam into chaos. When John Kennedy came into office, there had been 2,000 American "advisors" in Vietnam; by November 1963, there were 16,000. Kennedy was committed to propping up the South Vietnamese government as a bulwark against communism, but it remains unclear how far he was prepared to commit the United States to military conflict. At times the president spoke of pulling out of the country altogether after the 1964 U.S. election; at other times he spoke forcefully of the "domino theory," the belief that once South Vietnam fell to the Communists, the other nations of Southeast Asia would tumble into their hands like a line of dominoes.

Whether or not Jack Kennedy would personally have supported a war in Vietnam, the tone of his administration paved the way toward greater involvement. His confidence that the United States was invincible, that it was destined to combat communism, led some people to believe that America could solve the world's problems. That way of thinking, shared by many Americans, eventually cost the lives of more than 50,000 members of the United States military in Vietnam.

In mid-November of 1963, John Kennedy was poised between two positions on world affairs. He was tottering on the edge of deeper military involvement in Southeast Asia, yet his experience in the world theater had helped him to move away from the stark vision of good and evil that had inspired the Bay of Pigs invasion. He had managed to negotiate the test ban treaty, moving the world one step back from nuclear war, though he continued to support large increases in military spending. He was in a position, as no other president had ever been, to help dispel the climate of fear, to reject the idea that the United States could police the world. It will never be certain whether Kennedy would have been able to move the world toward the ideal of peace that he spoke of so eloquently in a series of speeches earlier that year.

"What kind of peace do I mean?" he had asked in June. "Not a Pax Americana enforced on the world by American weapons of war. Not the peace of the grave or the security of the slave. I am talking about genuine peace, the kind of peace that makes life on earth worth living, the kind that enables men and nations to grow and to hope and to build a better life for their children—not merely peace for Americans but peace for all men and women—not merely peace in our time but peace for all time."

9

Legacy

**You may see their trunks arching in the woods
Years afterwards**

At 5:59 P.M. on Friday, November 22, 1963, *Air Force One* landed in the dark autumn evening at Andrews Air Force Base outside Washington, D.C. Dave Powers, Kenny O'Donnell, and Larry O'Brien placed the casket carrying John Kennedy's body on the plane's hydraulic lift. An honor guard of six men carried it to a waiting ambulance. At the airport, Lyndon Johnson, who had been sworn in as the thirty-sixth president of the United States aboard the aircraft, told the public, "I will do my best. That is all I can do. I ask for your help—and God's." The peaceful transition of office was accomplished.

The president's distraught brother Robert boarded the plane and rushed to Jackie. The two of them followed the casket off the plane and rode with it to Bethesda Naval Hospital, where an autopsy on the body was performed. At 4:23 A.M., Jackie, still wearing the bloodstained suit, walked beside her husband's flag-draped casket as it was carried into the East Room of the White House; there an honor guard continued the vigil.

The president's mother was in Hyannis Port when she heard the news. At first she was confused by the reports; but when Bobby telephoned, she knew Jack was dead. He was the third of her children to meet a violent death.

"Sometimes I wonder if there is something about my family that invites violence," she later reflected.

In his bedroom the president's father, paralyzed by a stroke and unable to speak, motioned to his youngest son to turn on the television set. Teddy, now a senator elected to Jack's seat, hesitated and then turned it on. It began to flicker and he yanked the plug from the socket. He gathered his strength and told his father the devastating news.

In the two days following the president's death, with the nation in the throes of grief and grueling self-examination, a bizarre series of events took place in Dallas. On Saturday, a formal charge of the assassination of President John F. Kennedy was lodged against Lee Harvey Oswald. The next day, as he was being transferred to a higher-security jail, in the bright light of television cameras, a man darted out and shot Oswald in the abdomen. Millions of people witnessed the murder on television screens across the nation. Oswald died shortly afterward at the same hospital where the president had been taken and where Governor Connally was just recovering consciousness.

Jack Ruby, a nightclub owner, was immediately arrested and charged with Oswald's murder. Although Ruby insisted that he had killed Oswald in rage over Kennedy's murder, it still remains unclear why, or even whether, Lee Harvey Oswald killed the president and whether Ruby's act was self-motivated. Oswald made no confession. He did not seem to hold any hatred for President Kennedy.

The final judgment about the assassination is yet to be pronounced. Many theories persist about why Lee Harvey Oswald murdered Jack Kennedy and whether he acted alone or as part of a conspiracy linked either to international politics or to the underworld of crime and drugs. Some people believe that Governor Connally was the target. The conclusion of the Warren Commission, appointed to examine the evidence, was that Lee Harvey Oswald acted alone and that Jack Ruby killed him to save Jackie from the ordeal of Oswald's trial. The act may have provided the enraged Ruby with personal catharsis or relief, but it denied the nation any possibility of collective ca-

Lyndon Baines Johnson, standing between his wife and Mrs. Kennedy, takes the oath of office aboard *Air Force One*. (November 22, 1963)

tharsis in the tragedy. The Warren Commission left many unanswered questions that have led to countless speculations about the assassination and about the subsequent murder of Lee Harvey Oswald.

While thousands of grieving mourners solemnly wound their way past the coffin, which had been placed in the Capitol rotunda, a group of schoolchildren in Dallas, imitating the adult hatred that surrounded them, applauded the news of the president's death. Not everyone in Dallas shared their sentiments: "I hope you guys don't think too bad of Dallas," a salesman said to a reporter.

At one o'clock on Monday afternoon, Jackie stood at the north portico of the White House, with Caroline and John, Jr., on either side of her. In their blue coats, the children watched the honor guard lift the casket onto the artillery caisson. Three pairs of dapple-gray horses drew the carriage past the White House to St. Matthew's Cathedral. Three guards of honor rode the horses in the left row. By custom, the horses in the right row were saddled but without riders. The horse-drawn carriage was followed by a riderless horse, high black boots reversed in the stirrups, symbolizing the warrior who would not mount again. Three-year-old John, Jr., saluted his father's coffin from the steps of the cathedral. Caroline reached out to comfort her anguished mother. Days later, Caroline asked her nanny if God would give her daddy something to do in heaven; John, Jr., wondered when his dad was coming home.

Side by side with the grief, hatred and violence smoldered consciously and unconsciously throughout the nation. John Kennedy once said that there were only two days in recent history so memorable that people could recall exactly where they were at the time: the day Pearl Harbor was attacked by the Japanese and the day Franklin Delano Roosevelt died. In the autumn of 1963 a third day was etched into the hearts of that generation of Americans.

While he was president, Jack Kennedy had reflected on what he might do after his years in office were over. "Whether I serve one or two terms in the presidency," he said, "I will find myself at the end of that period at what might be called the awkward age—too old to begin a new career and too young to write my memoirs." He contemplated many possibilities for the future: writing, teaching, returning to Congress. He also thought about becoming a university president, perhaps of Harvard.

"It can be said of him, as of few men in a like position," wrote author E. B. White, "that he did not fear the weather, and did not trim his sails, but

The Kennedy family at the president's funeral. (November 25, 1963)

instead challenged the wind itself, to improve its direction and to cause it to blow more softly and more kindly over the world and its people."

In a large segment of the American population, Kennedy awakened a feeling of the nation's heroic promise and an awareness of its humane mission. In restoring dignity to politics, Jack Kennedy made government service seem honorable again. As the first Roman Catholic president, he provided an example to people of every religion to seek the highest office in the land.

The years following the assassination were among the most challenging and frightening in United States history. Both the vitality of those years and the divisions that rocked the country over civil rights and Vietnam owed something to the Kennedy presidency.

During his brief thousand days in office, Kennedy's actual accomplishments fell short of his ambitions. Historians and others criticized his caution on civil rights, his militancy in response to Soviet power, his snail's pace in attacking poverty, his escalation of troops in Vietnam.

On the other hand, the pace of the civil rights movement quickened during his presidency, and as a result, people felt empowered. The civil rights bill that Kennedy proposed in the aftermath of the Birmingham crisis eventually became law under the leadership of a southerner, President Lyndon Johnson. Through the Voting Rights Act of 1964 and other civil rights legislation, blacks finally won legal backing to protect their basic rights as citizens. But the assassination of Martin Luther King, Jr., in 1968 served as a stark reminder that full equality and brotherhood remained elusive goals.

One of Kennedy's greatest contributions was the Nuclear Test Ban Treaty, which helped pave the way toward extensive arms-reduction negotiations between the superpowers. The Cold War that loomed over John Kennedy's political career gradually thawed. In 1989, twenty-six years after Kennedy declared, *"Ich bin ein Berliner,"* East Germany opened its borders, and Germans from both sides clambered gleefully over the wall that for more than a quarter century symbolized the barrier between East and West.

Much of Kennedy's faith in public service survived the chaos of the 1960s.

The Peace Corps continued strong, and a domestic service program, Volunteers in Service to America (VISTA), established in 1964, sent thousands of people to fight poverty within the United States. Lyndon Johnson's War on Poverty, which expanded the government's commitment to the poor, built on many of Kennedy's initiatives. In 1969, astronaut Neil Armstrong took his "one giant leap for mankind" and, by setting foot on the moon, fulfilled the pledge that Kennedy made in the aftermath of the Bay of Pigs.

The conflict in Vietnam, still in the background during Kennedy's last years, haunted the nation. The battle over Southeast Asia consumed the United States for more than ten years. Across the country, young people in high school and college, and many of their parents, vigorously protested the war, and the pride in the United States that John Kennedy promoted came under bitter attack.

During his short tenure in office, Kennedy grew immensely in his understanding of complex issues and processes. He was not the same man in 1963 that he was in 1961. Nor were the American people the same. In a nation that had faced a long depression, a world war, and other tribulations at home and abroad, John Kennedy awakened possibilities that had long been dormant. People became exhilarated by the idea of new frontiers in space, and of economic and social justice.

Kennedy's leadership his view of power and his conception of virtue—was a synthesis of boldness and restraint. He learned that maneuvering a bill through Congress was a long, arduous, and deliberate process that involved compromise. He believed in the power of reconciliation over confrontation.

John Kennedy was always drawn to concepts of courage, understanding one facet of courage as Hemingway's "grace under pressure"—the bullfighter's apparent ease in the face of a charging bull—a phrase that Kennedy had made his own in the book *Profiles in Courage*.

At the time of his death, many people believed that life had come easy to Jack Kennedy, that he had achieved success at little personal cost. Just as reality became clouded in the lives of George Washington and Abraham Lincoln, John Kennedy's life was obscured, the man himself lost—the frail boy who battled with his older brother for his father's esteem, the gawky young veteran who knocked on doors in Charlestown, the untried new president who wrestled with the cares of state. Few people understood that Kennedy's view of himself and the world was shaped by loss, by grief, and by pain.

In early January 1961, in his farewell speech to the Massachusetts legislature, Kennedy stated that history measures success and failure in political office by the answers to four questions: "First, were we truly men of courage? . . . Second, were we truly men of judgment? . . . Third, were we truly men of integrity? . . . Finally, were we truly men of dedication? . . . ."

By courage, Kennedy meant more than bravery in battle. He meant standing up for beliefs despite the consequences. Judgment, Kennedy interpreted as wisdom and the candor to own up to mistakes and learn from them. By integrity, he implied never sacrificing principles to expedience. By dedication, he meant selfless commitment to the public good, without compromise to private aim or desire. Kennedy knew that he did not unfailingly live up to these expectations, but his questions indicate the high standards by which he wished to be judged.

In his speeches, books, and press conferences, President Kennedy had written his own epitaph countless times; perhaps the most memorable came from his inaugural address—"Ask not what your country can do for you. Ask what you can do for your country." It was Kennedy's rallying cry to the people of the United States and was a summons to move beyond apathy and indifference. "The only thing necessary for the triumph of evil," he observed, quoting Edmund Burke, "is for good men to do nothing." If you want things to be better, he remonstrated, you must contribute to making them better. His greatest legacy was this goading to action, this deep belief in the power of the individual to change the existing order.

John Kennedy lived a life of paradoxes. The image of him sailing, playing football, golf, and tennis—and wearing no hat, no coat, even in the coldest weather—is incongruous with his private world of unrelenting pain. He was confident; still, he struggled with the insecurity of walking in the footsteps of his favored older brother. He was a dedicated family man, yet he was unfaithful to his wife. He depended on a close circle of family and friends but faced the toughest crises in his life and presidency alone. A man of reflection as well as action, he appeared at once vulnerable and indomitable.

Among friends he could curse with the best, but in public he was given to eloquence. He worked tirelessly on behalf of decency and justice and yet he was just beginning to comprehend the anger and desperation of those who had been denied their basic rights as citizens. He set the highest standards for himself and for his country, even while he encouraged the excesses of competition. He sought peace, and he brought the nation to the brink of war. He was full of wit and energy and life, and yet he was preoccupied with tragedy and death. In his brief life, John Fitzgerald Kennedy traveled a course between the daylight and the darkness.

A man of the sea. (America's Cup yacht races, 1962)

Afterword

Our research for the film documentary *JFK: In His Own Words* (Home Box Office) was the catalyst for this biography; our perception was that many young people, if they knew Jack Kennedy at all, viewed him as someone born with a silver spoon in his mouth, someone who never had to work hard at anything. We wanted to bring a different Kennedy to life: the private Kennedy, the man behind the myth, the poet and the politician, the idealist and the pragmatist, the man of reflection as well as the man of action.

We would like to express our gratitude to several people who were instrumental in the development of the biography. First, we would like to thank Peter W. Kunhardt, executive producer of the film documentary; and Dorothy Briley, formerly at Lothrop, Lee & Shepard Books, for her belief in the book itself.

The architecturally splendid John F. Kennedy Library in Boston became a home away from home during more than three years of research. We inhabited mainly two rooms: a windowless media room on the third floor, and a fourth-floor reading room with a sweeping view of Boston Harbor. To the staff of the Kennedy Library we would like to express a special thank you, particularly to Alan Goodrich, audiovisual archivist, and Ron Whealan, librarian, for their assistance. We would also like to thank Sam Rubin, education specialist, and Sheldon Stern, historian, for their thoughtful readings of the manuscript.

We owe a great debt to Herbert A. Selenkow, M.D., Harvard Medical School, for his counsel on Addison's disease and other ailments that plagued Jack Kennedy, and much gratitude to Lolly Selenkow for her ongoing and generous support.

At Lothrop, Lee & Shepard we would like to thank Susan Pearson, editor-in-chief, for her encouragement, and Judit Bodnar, senior editor, for her unflagging commitment.

We are especially grateful to Ruth Gordon for her meticulous reading of the manuscript and wise advice and perseverance in seeing the book through several drafts. The title of Ruth's recent anthology of poems, *Time is the Longest Distance*, suggests the reserves of patience that were necessary to see this project through from start to finish.

Finally, we would like to thank Maggie Stern Terris for her perceptive response to the book and unfailing trust in its authors.

Barbara Harrison and Daniel Terris

Cambridge, Massachusetts
September 1991

Sources of Information About
John F. Kennedy

Among several books about Kennedy's prepresidential years, two are indispensable: James MacGregor Burns's *John Fitzgerald Kennedy: A Political Profile* and Doris Kearns Goodwin's *The Fitzgeralds and the Kennedys: An American Saga.* Burns's book, published in 1960, holds up surprisingly well over time. Goodwin's book, published in 1987, is more ambitious in scope. Goodwin examines the rise of the Fitzgeralds and the Kennedys from the slums of Boston to the White House. An absorbing book, it is reliable, judicious, and full of fresh perceptions about John Kennedy's formative years. As a contribution to Kennedy scholarship, *The Fitzgeralds and the Kennedys* is a landmark book.

The Making of the President 1960, by journalist Theodore H. White, captures the heartbeat of the 1960 presidential campaign.

Several of John Kennedy's inner circle of advisors have contributed to Kennedy scholarship. Theodore C. Sorensen, with whom Jack Kennedy formed an almost perfect alliance, wrote a book in 1965 called *Kennedy*. More recently, he edited *"Let the Word Go Forth": The Speeches, Statements, and Writings of John F. Kennedy, 1947 to 1963*, an invaluable collection of Kennedy's speeches. *Johnny, We Hardly Knew Ye: Memories of John Fitzgerald Kennedy*, by Kenneth P. O'Donnell and David F. Powers with Joe McCarthy, is an affectionate portrait of the president by men who knew and loved him well.

In *Of Kennedys and Kings: Making Sense of the Sixties*, Harris Wofford, one of

Kennedy's civil-rights advisors, presents a balanced view of the president's accomplishments in office. In *Parting the Waters: America in the King Years, 1954–1963*, Taylor Branch paints intriguing portraits of John Kennedy and Martin Luther King, Jr., that provide new insights into their relationship. Herbert S. Parmet's well-documented, dispassionate portrayal, *JFK: The Presidency of John F. Kennedy*, is especially helpful in demythologizing the presidential years.

A fascinating book by Harvey Rachlin is also a vital research tool: *The Kennedys: A Chronological History, 1823–Present*. An almanac of valuable information, the book includes charts, photographs, and timelines.

John Fitzgerald Kennedy: As We Remember Him is an excellent collection of photographs and anecdotes contributed by family and friends, with an introductory essay by Robert Kennedy. Rich with biographical source material in the form of letters, conversations, and reminiscences, the book reveals a great deal about the inner world of the president from the time he was a small boy. Other books that reflect on Jack's early years include Rose Fitzgerald Kennedy's autobiography, *Times to Remember*; Hank Searls's biography of Jack's older brother, *The Lost Prince: Young Joe, the Forgotten Kennedy*; and Lynne McTaggart's biography of Kathleen Kennedy, *Kathleen Kennedy: Her Life and Times*.

The president's assassination is covered in William Manchester's *The Death of a President*, a fully researched account, and in *Four Days*, a historical documentation compiled by United Press International and the editors of *American Heritage*. The latter contains eyewitness accounts of the assassination, reactions from around the world, and eulogies for the slain president.

The film documentaries *JFK: In His Own Words* (HBO, 1988) and *Bobby Kennedy: In His Own Words* (HBO, 1990), produced by Peter W. Kunhardt, contain stirring personal glimpses of John F. Kennedy and Robert Kennedy, including audio tapes and film footage not previously available to the public. The companion book, *Life in Camelot: The Kennedy Era*, edited by Philip B. Kunhardt, is a treasure trove of photographic images of the times.

For those who wish to pursue certain topics in more depth, the single best source of information is the John F. Kennedy Library in Boston. Its collection of books about Kennedy and his era is comprehensive, as is its collection of personal papers of Kennedy family members and those associated with the presidential administration. Of particular interest is the oral history collection, including more than one thousand transcribed interviews with family, friends, colleagues, and White House employees including the doorman, the electrician, and the upholsterer. The audiovisual archives contain over 100,000 photographs, as well as audiotapes, home movies, and stock footage from television networks.

Of course, a person is revealed as much by the words he writes and speaks as by his actions, and therefore nothing can take the place of the president's own words in books such as *Profiles in Courage*, *As We Remember Joe*, and the aforementioned *"Let the Word Go Forth."*

Selected Bibliography

Branch, Taylor. *Parting the Waters: America in the King Years, 1954–1963*. New York: Simon & Schuster, 1988.

Burns, James MacGregor. *John Fitzgerald Kennedy: A Political Profile*. New York: Harcourt, Brace, and World, 1960.

Collier, Peter, and David Horowitz. *The Kennedys: An American Drama*. New York: Summit, 1984.

Goodwin, Doris Kearns. *The Fitzgeralds and the Kennedys: An American Saga*. New York: Simon & Schuster, 1987.

Kennedy, John F. *Profiles in Courage*. New York: Harper, 1956.

Kennedy, John F., ed. *As We Remember Joe*. Cambridge, Massachusetts: Privately printed, 1945.

Kennedy, Rose. *Times to Remember*. New York: Doubleday, 1974.

Kunhardt, Philip D., ed. *Life in Camelot: The Kennedy Era*. Boston: Little, Brown, 1988.

O'Donnell, Kenneth P., and David F. Powers (with Joe McCarthy). *Johnny, We Hardly Knew Ye: Memories of John Fitzgerald Kennedy*. Boston: Little, Brown, 1972.

Manchester, William. *The Death of a President*. New York: Harper/Perennial, 1988.

McTaggart, Lynne. *Kathleen Kennedy: Her Life and Times*. New York: Dial, 1983.

Meyers, Joan, ed. *John Fitzgerald Kennedy; As We Remember Him*. New York: Atheneum, 1965.

Parmet, Herbert S. *JFK: The Presidency of John F. Kennedy*. New York: Dial, 1983.

Rachlin, Harvey. *The Kennedys: A Chronological History, 1823–Present*. New York: World Almanac, 1986.

Schlesinger, Arthur M. Jr. *A Thousand Days: John F. Kennedy in the White House*. Boston: Houghton Mifflin, 1965.

Searls, Hank. *The Lost Prince: Young Joe, The Forgotten Kennedy*. New York: World, 1969.

Sorensen, Theodore C. *Kennedy*. New York: Harper, 1965.

Sorensen, Theodore C., ed. *"Let the Word Go Forth": The Speeches, Statements, and Writings of John F. Kennedy, 1947 to 1963*. New York: Delacorte, 1988.

White, Theodore. *The Making of the President 1960*. New York: Atheneum, 1961.

Wofford, Harris. *Of Kennedys and Kings: Making Sense of the Sixties*. New York: Farrar, Straus & Giroux, 1980.

Four Days: The Historical Record of the Death of President Kennedy. Compiled by United Press International and *American Heritage Magazine*. New York: American Heritage, 1964.

A *Chronology of Events*

AUGUST 20, 1914   Joseph P. Kennedy buys home at 83 Beals Street, Brookline, Massachusetts.

OCTOBER 7, 1914   Rose Elizabeth Fitzgerald and Joseph Patrick Kennedy marry.

JULY 25, 1915   Joseph Patrick Kennedy, Jr., is born in Hull, Massachusetts.

APRIL 6, 1917   The United States enters World War I.

MAY 29, 1917   John Fitzgerald Kennedy is born on Beals Street in Brookline.

NOVEMBER 7, 1917   Bolsheviks overthrow Kerensky and establish Soviet socialist republic.

SEPTEMBER 13, 1918   Rosemary Kennedy is born on Beals Street.

NOVEMBER 11, 1918   Armistice, ending World War I, takes effect.

FEBRUARY 20, 1920   Kathleen Agnes Kennedy is born on Beals Street.

MARCH 16, 1920   Joseph Kennedy purchases home on corner of Naples and Abbottsford roads in Brookline (52 Abbottsford Road).

AUGUST 26, 1920   The Nineteenth Amendment, giving women the right to vote, is adopted.

JULY 10, 1921   Eunice Mary Kennedy is born at 52 Abbottsford Road, Brookline.

SEPTEMBER 12, 1921   John enters kindergarten at the Edward Devotion School in Brookline.

MAY 6, 1924   Patricia Kennedy is born on Abbottsford Road in Brookline.

NOVEMBER 20, 1925   Robert Francis Kennedy is born on Abbottsford Road.

FEBRUARY 7, 1926   Joseph Kennedy enters the motion-picture production business, buying control of Film Book Offices (FBO).

MAY 20, 1927   Capt. Charles A. Lindbergh leaves New York in the *Spirit of St. Louis* for the first nonstop airplane flight across the Atlantic Ocean.

SEPTEMBER 1927   The Kennedy family moves from Massachusetts to Riverdale in the Bronx, New York.

SEPTEMBER 27, 1927   John enters the fifth grade at Riverdale Country School.

FEBRUARY 20, 1928   Jean Ann Kennedy is born at St. Margaret's Hospital in Dorchester, Massachusetts.

NOVEMBER 6, 1928   Joseph and Rose Kennedy purchase land in Hyannis Port, Massachusetts.

MAY 4, 1929   The Kennedys purchase a home at 294 Pondfield Road in the Westchester community of Bronxville, New York.

MAY 18, 1929   Patrick Joseph Kennedy, 71, dies of cancer at Deaconess Hospital in Boston, Masssachusetts.

SEPTEMBER 30, 1929   Joe, Jr., 14, enters his freshman year at the Choate School in Wallingford, Connecticut.

OCTOBER 29, 1929   U.S. stock-market prices plummet, precipitating the Great Depression. Over the next several years, there is much economic instability as banks fail and depositors panic.

SEPTEMBER 24, 1930   John, 13, enters the eighth grade at Canterbury, a boarding school in New Milford, Connecticut.

SEPTEMBER 19, 1931   John, 14, enters his freshman year at Choate School.

FEBRUARY 22, 1932   Edward Moore Kennedy is born at St. Margaret's Hospital in Dorchester, Massachusetts.

JUNE 10, 1932   Joe, Jr., 17, graduates from Choate.

MARCH 4, 1933   Franklin Delano Roosevelt is sworn in as the 32d president of the United States.

JUNE 30, 1933   The Kennedys purchase a home at 1095 North Ocean Boulevard in Palm Beach, Florida.

JULY 2, 1934   Joseph Kennedy is named to his first major political job as chairman of the Securities and Exchange Commission (SEC).

SEPTEMBER 24, 1934   Joe, Jr., 19, begins his freshman year at Harvard College in Cambridge, Massachusetts.

JUNE 8, 1935   John, 18, graduates from Choate.

OCTOBER 26, 1935   Because of illness, John enters his freshman year at Princeton University late.

DECEMBER 12, 1935   Illness forces John to withdraw from Princeton.

SEPTEMBER 28, 1936   John, 19, enters Harvard as a freshman.

JANUARY 5, 1938   President Roosevelt appoints Joseph Kennedy ambassador to Great Britain; he assumes his official duties on March 8, 1938.

JUNE 23, 1938   Joe, Jr., 22, graduates from Harvard.

SEPTEMBER 1, 1939   Germany invades Poland; World War II begins.

SEPTEMBER 3, 1939   In a speech before the House of Commons, Prime Minister Neville Chamberlain announces that Great Britain is at war with Germany. John, Joe, Jr., Kathleen, and their parents are in attendance when the announcement is made.

JUNE 20, 1940   John graduates *cum laude* from Harvard; his honors thesis, "Appeasement at Munich," is awarded a *magna cum laude*.

AUGUST 1, 1940   *Why England Slept*, by the 23-year-old John Kennedy, is published by Wilfred Funk, Inc.; the book is an adaptation of his Harvard thesis.

DECEMBER 2, 1940   Joseph Kennedy formally resigns as ambassador to England.

JUNE 24, 1941   Joe, Jr., joins the United States Naval Reserve as a seaman, second class.

OCTOBER 8, 1941   John is appointed an ensign in the U.S. Naval Reserve.

DECEMBER 7, 1941   Japan attacks Pearl Harbor, Hawaii.

DECEMBER 8, 1941   The United States declares war on Japan.

DECEMBER 11, 1941   The United States declares war on Germany and Italy.

JULY 1942   Rosemary Kennedy takes up permanent residence in St. Coletta's School in Jefferson, Wisconsin, after a brain operation in 1941 leaves her helpless.

AUGUST 2, 1943   PT-109, commanded by Lt. (jg) John F. Kennedy, is sunk by a Japanese destroyer in the South Pacific.

MAY 6, 1944   In a civil ceremony in London, Kathleen Kennedy, 24, marries William John Robert Cavendish, 26, Lord Hartington.

MAY 31, 1944   John enters U.S. Naval Hospital in Chelsea, Massachusetts, because of lingering back trouble caused by the collision and sinking of PT-109.

JUNE 12, 1944   John receives the Navy and Marine Corps Medal for "extremely heroic conduct as Commanding Officer of Motor Torpedo Boat 109."

AUGUST 12, 1944 Lt. Joseph P. Kennedy, Jr., 29, is killed on a mission when his PB-44 drone Liberator, loaded with over 21,000 pounds of TNT, explodes over the English Channel.

SEPTEMBER 10, 1944 William, Lord Hartington, 26, is killed in action in Heppen, Belgium.

APRIL 1945 *As We Remember Joe*, a book of recollections of Joseph P. Kennedy, Jr., is privately printed; John compiled the essays and contributed to the memorial tribute to his brother.

APRIL 12, 1945 Franklin Delano Roosevelt dies; Harry S Truman becomes the 33d president of the United States.

APRIL 25–JUNE 16, 1945 As a reporter for the International News Service, John covers the San Francisco conference that drafts the United Nations Charter.

MAY 7–8, 1945 Germany surrenders, unconditionally ending the European part of World War II.

AUGUST 6, 1945 The United States drops the first atomic bomb on Hiroshima, Japan. More than 80,000 Japanese are killed.

AUGUST 9, 1945 Second U.S. atomic bomb is dropped on Nagasaki.

AUGUST 14, 1945 Japan surrenders, and the Asian part of World War II ends.

APRIL 25, 1946 John Kennedy announces his candidacy for the Democratic nomination to Congress from Massachusetts's Eleventh Congressional District.

JUNE 18, 1946 John defeats nine other candidates to win his first election, the Democratic nomination to Congress from the Eleventh Congressional District.

NOVEMBER 5, 1946 Winning over 70% of the popular vote, John F. Kennedy is elected to his first political office, United States Congressman from Massachusetts.

JANUARY 3, 1947 Kennedy, 29, is sworn in as a U.S. Congressman.

OCTOBER 11, 1947 A hospitalization in England cuts short Kennedy's European tour.

MAY 13, 1948 Kathleen Kennedy Cavendish, Lady Hartington, is killed in a plane crash in southern France.

NOVEMBER 2, 1948 Kennedy is elected to a second term from the Eleventh Congressional District of Massachusetts.

JANUARY 3, 1949 Kennedy begins his second term of office as a U.S. Congressman; he continues to serve as a member of the District of Columbia Committee and the Education and Labor Committee.

JUNE 17, 1950 Robert Kennedy marries Ethel Skakel at St. Mary's Church in Greenwich, Connecticut.

JUNE 25, 1950 North Korean troops invade the Republic of Korea. The United Nations, with military support from the United States, intervenes.

OCTOBER 2, 1950 John Francis "Honey Fitz" Fitzgerald dies of a heart attack in his apartment at the Hotel Bellevue in Boston.

NOVEMBER 7, 1950 Kennedy is elected to a third term in the House of Representatives, defeating his Republican opponent by a wide margin.

JANUARY 3, 1951 The Eighty-second Congress convenes; Kennedy, 33, begins his third term as a congressman.

APRIL 24, 1952 John Kennedy announces his candidacy for the U.S. Senate.

NOVEMBER 4, 1952 In his bid for a seat in the Senate, Kennedy defeats Henry Cabot Lodge, Jr. On the same day, Dwight David Eisenhower is elected the 34th president of the United States. Richard Milhous Nixon becomes vice president.

JANUARY 3, 1953 Kennedy, 35, begins his first term as United States Senator from Massachusetts.

SEPTEMBER 12, 1953 In St. Mary's Church in Newport, Rhode Island, John Fitzgerald Kennedy, 36, marries Jacqueline Lee Bouvier, 24.

MAY 17, 1954 In a unanimous decision on *Brown v. Board of Education of Topeka, Kansas*, the Supreme Court rules that racial segregation in public schools is illegal.

OCTOBER 21, 1954 At the Hospital for Special Surgery in New York, Kennedy undergoes spinal surgery.

DECEMBER 2, 1954 The U.S. Senate votes 67 to 22 to censure Senator Joseph R. McCarthy. Recuperating from his operation, Kennedy is not present to vote.

DECEMBER 21, 1954 Accompanied by his wife, Kennedy leaves for his family's home in Palm Beach, Florida, to convalesce.

FEBRUARY 11, 1955 Kennedy undergoes a second spinal operation in New York; during several months of convalescence (again in Palm Beach), Kennedy writes *Profiles in Courage*.

MAY 25, 1955 Kennedy returns to his office in Washington, D.C., to resume his duties as senator.

DECEMBER 5, 1955 Blacks in Montgomery, Alabama, begin a year-long boycott of the city's bus system.

JANUARY 1, 1956 *Profiles in Courage* is published by Harper and Brothers.

AUGUST 16, 1956 Senator Kennedy delivers Adlai E. Stevenson's presidential nomination speech at the Democratic National Convention in Chicago; Stevenson won his party's nomination on the first ballot.

AUGUST 17, 1956 Kennedy narrowly loses the Democratic vice-presidential nomination to Estes Kefauver but emerges as a national figure.

AUGUST 23, 1956 In Newport, Rhode Island, Jacqueline Kennedy gives birth prematurely to her first child, a stillborn baby girl.

NOVEMBER 6, 1956 President Dwight D. Eisenhower and Vice-President Richard M. Nixon are reelected.

FEBRUARY 26, 1957 Senator John L. McClellan opens Senate hearings on labor racketeering in the International Brotherhood of Teamsters. Robert Kennedy serves as chief counsel of the Senate labor rackets committee, and John Kennedy serves on the committee.

MAY 6, 1957 John Kennedy's *Profiles in Courage* is awarded the 1957 Pulitzer Prize for a biography or autobiography.

OCTOBER 4, 1957 The Soviet Union heralds the space age with *Sputnik I,* a 184-pound artificial satellite.

NOVEMBER 27, 1957 Caroline Bouvier Kennedy is born to Jacqueline, 28, and John Kennedy, 40, at the New York Lying-In Hospital–Cornell Medical Center.

NOVEMBER 4, 1958 By the largest margin in the history of Massachusetts, Kennedy is elected to a second term in the U.S. Senate.

JANUARY 1, 1959 Fidel Castro topples dictator Fulgencio Batista y Zaldiva, to become premier of Cuba.

JANUARY 3, 1959 Kennedy begins his second term as a Massachusetts senator.

JANUARY 2, 1960 Kennedy, 42, formally announces his candidacy for the presidency of the United States.

MARCH 5, 1960 Senator Kennedy wins New Hampshire's Democratic presidential primary.

APRIL 5, 1960 Kennedy defeats Senator Hubert Humphrey of Minnesota to win the Wisconsin Democratic presidential primary.

MAY 10, 1960 Hubert Humphrey withdraws from the presidential race after an upset victory by Kennedy in West Virginia's presidential primary.

JULY 13, 1960 At the Democratic National Convention in Los Angeles, Kennedy wins the presidential nomination of the Democratic party on the first ballot.

JULY 14, 1960 Senator Lyndon Baines Johnson is selected vice-presidential nominee at the Los Angeles convention.

SEPTEMBER 12, 1960 Kennedy speaks to the Greater Houston Ministerial Association at the Rice Hotel in Houston, Texas; he clarifies his position on religion and politics.

SEPTEMBER 26, 1960   John F. Kennedy debates Richard M. Nixon, Republican candidate for president, in the first of four televised debates. The other debates take place on October 7, October 13, and October 21 of the same year.

OCTOBER 19, 1960   Martin Luther King, Jr., is arrested in Atlanta for civil-rights protests.

OCTOBER 26, 1960   Kennedy telephones Coretta Scott King in Georgia and offers his help.

NOVEMBER 8, 1960   John Fitzgerald Kennedy is elected 35th president of the United States, defeating Nixon by a narrow margin.

NOVEMBER 25, 1960   John Fitzgerald Kennedy, Jr., is born to Jacqueline and John Kennedy at Georgetown University Hospital in Washington, D.C.

DECEMBER 16, 1960   President-elect Kennedy announces that he has appointed his brother Robert attorney general.

JANUARY 9, 1961   President-elect Kennedy delivers a farewell speech to the Massachusetts legislature.

JANUARY 20, 1961   Kennedy, 43, is inaugurated President of the United States

FEBRUARY 1, 1961   The president holds his first live televised press conference.

MARCH 1, 1961   Kennedy signs a bill to establish the Peace Corps, a volunteer corps of skilled young people to be sent to developing countries all over the world to teach and serve the people.

MARCH 8, 1961   Kennedy establishes the President's Committee on Equal Employment Opportunity; the executive order guarantees equal access to government jobs to all citizens, regardless of creed or color.

MARCH 13, 1961   Kennedy establishes the Alliance for Progress, a program aimed at aiding the economic development of Latin American countries

MARCH 28, 1961   In a special message, Kennedy asks Congress for a major defense appropriation to ensure national security.

MARCH 29, 1961   The president signs an executive order establishing a Council on Youth Fitness.

APRIL 17, 1961   An attempt to overthrow Cuba's Premier Fidel Castro fails; Cuban exiles under the direction of the U.S. Government are killed or captured at the Bay of Pigs, Cuba.

MAY 5, 1961   The United States sends its first astronaut into space.

MAY 11, 1961   The United States sends 400 Special Forces troops and 100 other advisors to Vietnam.

MAY 16, 1961   Freedom Riders are attacked by vicious white mobs in Anniston and Birmingham, Alabama.

MAY 20, 1961   A busload of Freedom Riders is attacked by a mob of armed whites in Montgomery, Alabama; Attorney General Robert Kennedy sends 400 federal marshals to Montgomery.

JUNE 3–4, 1961   The president meets with Soviet Premier Nikita Khrushchev in Vienna about such topics as nuclear testing, disarmament, and Southeast Asia.

AUGUST 13, 1961   In East Berlin, Germany, the Berlin Wall is built, and the border between East Berlin and West Berlin is closed.

AUGUST 22, 1961   The first of a series of concerts performed by young people for young people is held at the White House.

SEPTEMBER 2, 1961   President Kennedy signs the Minimum Wage bill. President Kennedy and British Prime Minister Harold Macmillan invite Premier Nikita Khrushchev to accept their proposal banning nuclear testing; Khrushchev refuses.

SEPTEMBER 22, 1961   The Peace Corps Act is signed by Kennedy, permanently establishing the organization.

NOVEMBER 13, 1961   Following a White House dinner in honor of Puerto Rican Governor Luis Muñoz Marin and his wife, renowned cellist Pablo Casals performs in the East Room.

DECEMBER 16–17, 1961   President and Mrs. Kennedy make an official visit to San Juan, Puerto Rico; Venezuela; and Colombia.

JANUARY 18, 1962   Composer Igor Stravinsky and his wife are honored at a White House dinner.

FEBRUARY 1962   Major buildup of advisors starts in Vietnam; 12,000 U.S. military personnel are in the country by June.

FEBRUARY 20, 1962   Kennedy congratulates Lt. Col. John H. Glenn, Jr., for successfully orbiting the earth three times.

APRIL 29, 1962   President and Mrs. Kennedy host a dinner at the White House for 49 Nobel Prize winners.

SEPTEMBER 29, 1962   The president and Attorney General Robert Kennedy confer about crisis developing over James H. Meredith, Jr.'s efforts to enroll at the University of Mississippi; they try to negotiate a peaceful resolution with Mississippi Governor Ross R. Barnett.

SEPTEMBER 30, 1962 President Kennedy addresses the nation on radio and television, criticizing violence over James Meredith's attempt to enroll at the University of Mississippi. Kennedy encourages people to obey federal law; he sends federal marshals to Oxford, Mississippi, to escort Meredith into a dormitory.

OCTOBER 1, 1962 James Meredith formally enrolls at the University of Mississippi.

OCTOBER 16–28, 1962 Cuban Missile Crisis. Based on aerial photos showing Soviet missile bases in Cuba, on October 22 Kennedy announces a naval blockade of Cuba, "a strict quarantine on all offensive military equipment"; the United States threatens military action, and the U.S.S.R. removes its missile installations.

NOVEMBER 20, 1962 Kennedy signs an executive order barring discrimination in federal housing.

MARCH 22, 1963 President Kennedy urges states to pass the Twenty-fourth Amendment to the Constitution; the amendment prohibits poll taxes.

MAY 12, 1963 Civil disturbances in Birmingham, Alabama, prompt Kennedy to make an urgent appeal to the people of Birmingham to calm down and maintain order.

JUNE 10, 1963 Kennedy delivers a major address at American University on world peace and nuclear disarmament.

JUNE 11, 1963 Kennedy broadcasts a civil rights message to the nation.

JUNE 19, 1963 President Kennedy sends a bold, comprehensive civil rights bill to Congress.

JUNE 23–JULY 2, 1963 Kennedy visits West Germany, Ireland, England, and Italy; on June 26, he delivers his *"Ich bin ein Berliner"* speech in West Berlin.

JULY 25, 1963 The Soviet Union, Great Britain, and the United States agree on a limited nuclear test ban treaty.

AUGUST 7, 1963 Patrick Bouvier Kennedy is born prematurely to President and Mrs. Kennedy. The baby dies on August 9 and is buried on August 10 at Holyhood Cemetery in Brookline.

AUGUST 18, 1963 James Meredith graduates from the University of Mississippi.

AUGUST 28, 1963 A monumental civil rights demonstration takes place in Washington, D.C.; over 200,000 marchers assemble at the Lincoln Memorial, where Martin Luther King, Jr., delivers his "I have a dream" speech.

OCTOBER 10, 1963 The nuclear test ban treaty goes into effect.

OCTOBER 26, 1963   President Kennedy delivers a tribute to Robert Frost and to the arts at Amherst College in Amherst, Massachusetts, where he dedicates the new Robert Frost Memorial Library and receives an honorary Doctor of Law degree from the college.

NOVEMBER 1, 1963   A military coup topples President Ngo Dinh Diem's government in South Vietnam. Both Diem and his brother, Ngo Dinh Nhu, are assassinated.

NOVEMBER 22, 1963   President John Fitzgerald Kennedy, 46 years old, is assassinated in Dallas, Texas.

Source Notes

Page

All chapter epigraphs are from Robert Frost's poem "Birches," in *The Complete Poems of Robert Frost*, edited by Edward Connery Lathem (New York: Holt, Rinehart & Winston, 1969).

1   "My back feels better than it's felt in years": Kenneth P. O'Donnell and David F. Powers with Joe McCarthy, *Johnny, We Hardly Knew Ye: Memories of John Fitzgerald Kennedy* (Boston: Little, Brown, 1972; Pocket, 1973), p. 2.

3   ". . . so why worry about it?": O'Donnell and Powers, p. 26.

3   the lifeless bird: Charles Spalding, Oral History, John F. Kennedy Library, p. 3.

3   "You sure can't say Dallas doesn't love you, Mr. President": William Manchester, *The Death of a President* (New York: Harper, 1967; Harper Perennial, 1988), p. 153.

4   "a rag doll": O'Donnell and Powers, p. 29.

4   "they've killed my husband!": Manchester, *Death of a President*, p. 160; *Warren Commission Report*, p. 62.

5   "Let me alone": Manchester, *Death of a President*, p. 171.

7   "but I have lots of children": Gail Cameron, *Rose: A Biography of Rose Fitzgerald Kennedy* (New York: Putnam, 1971), p. 81.

12   "We want no losers around here. . . .": Lynne McTaggart, *Kathleen Kennedy: Her Life and Times* (New York: Dial, 1983), p. 1.

13   "Nothing trivial was ever discussed at the table. . . ."; Cameron, p. 85.

14   "could fight like fury": Rose Fitzgerald Kennedy, *Times to Remember* (New York: Doubleday, 1974; Bantam, 1975), p. 125.

14   "the mosquito was almost sure to die": Joan Meyers, ed., *John Fitzgerald Kennedy; As We Remember Him* (New York: Atheneum, 1965), p. vi.

15   "Pied Piper": Doris Kearns Goodwin, *The Fitzgeralds and the Kennedys: An American Saga* (New York: Simon & Schuster, 1987), p. 353.

16   "What the hell does someone have to do to become an American?": Peter Collier and David Horowitz, *The Kennedys: An American Drama* (New York: Summit, 1984), p. 21.

18   ". . . the glowing pride on his father's face": Goodwin, pp. 465–66.

21   Jack in the infirmary: Rose Fitzgerald Kennedy, p. 231.

21   Cablegram from Joe Kennedy: James MacGregor Burns, *John Fitzgerald Kennedy: A Political Profile* (New York: Harcourt, Brace & World, 1960), p. 42.

22   "I'm more or less interested in working sometime in my life for the government": John F. Kennedy, radio interview, Rochester, Minnesota, 1940; Recording MR 69-3, John F. Kennedy Library.

23   Shipboard seminars: Paul Fay, *The Pleasure of His Company* (New York: Harper & Row, 1966), p. 141.

25   "I'm shadowboxing a match the shadow is always going to win": Goodwin, pp. 698–99.

26   Jack's essay on Joe, Jr.: John F. Kennedy (ed.), *As We Remember Joe* (Cambridge, Mass.: privately published, 1945), p. 3.

26   "They came together in a way. . . ." Goodwin, p. 702.

33   "I'm only trying to fill his shoes": Joe McCarthy, *The Remarkable Kennedys* (New York: Dial, 1960), p. 120.

34   "If you want to talk to me about my family, I'll meet you outside": O'Donnell and Powers, p. 53.

34   JFK in the bath: William Manchester, *One Brief Shining Moment: Remembering Kennedy* (Boston: Little, Brown, 1983), p. 33.

36   "I never thought Jack had it in him": O'Donnell and Powers, p. 53.

37   "he hasn't got a year to live": Joan Blair and Clay Blair, Jr., *The Search for JFK* (New York: Putnam, 1976), p. 565.

39   "you will walk on a far larger canvas than I": Goodwin, pp. 746–47.

40   Joe's role in JFK's first campaign: David E. Koskoff, *Joseph P. Kennedy: A Life and Times* (Englewood Cliffs, N.J.: Prentice-Hall, 1974), p. 416.

44   He called her "from some oyster bar": Burns, p. 127.

46 "Rules for Visiting the Kennedys," *Saturday Evening Post*, Sept. 7, 1957.

47 "Just watching them wore me out": Ralph G. Martin, *A Hero for Our Time: An Intimate Story of the Kennedy Years* (New York: Fawcett, 1983), p. 77.

47 "he had a saltine at four in the afternoon and would get so thin": Jacqueline Kennedy, Recording MR-277, John F. Kennedy Library.

50 "I'd rather be dead": McCarthy, p. 151; O'Donnell and Powers, p. 113.

50 "We came close to losing him": Collier and Horowitz, p. 205.

53 JFK's vice-presidential bid: Goodwin, p. 784.

54 "I ought to be able to pick up all the marbles": O'Donnell and Powers, p. 146.

55 "Youth is not a presumption of vitality. . . .": John F. Kennedy, Recording MR-277, John F. Kennedy Library.

55 "just come out of my father's house": Theodore C. Sorensen, *Kennedy* (New York: Harper, 1965), p. 26.

55 "It's better not to know": John F. Kennedy, Recording MR-277, John F. Kennedy Library.

58 "religious dilemma": Philip B. Kunhardt, prod., *JFK: In His Own Words* (Home Box Office, 1988), draft edit.

59 "For while this year it may be a Catholic . . .": Theodore C. Sorensen, ed., *"Let the Word Go Forth": The Speeches, Statements, and Writings of John F. Kennedy, 1947 to 1963* (New York: Delacorte, 1988), p. 131.

59 "there are a lot of clods carrying cameras in this country": Stanley Tretick, Oral History, John F. Kennedy Library.

62 Selection of Johnson as vice-presidential nominee: Robert F. Kennedy, *Robert Kennedy: In His Own Words* (New York: Bantam, 1988), pp. 20–21.

62 "New Frontier" speech: Sorensen, *"Let the Word Go Forth,"* pp. 96–102.

66 Call to Coretta Scott King: Harris Wofford, *Of Kennedys and Kings: Making Sense of the Sixties* (New York: Farrar, Straus & Giroux, 1980), pp. 11–28; Taylor Branch, *Parting the Waters: America in the King Years, 1954–1963* (New York: Simon & Schuster, 1988), pp. 361–62.

67 "Well, we all have fathers, don't we?": Wofford, p. 28.

69 JFK on election day: Theodore White, *The Making of the President 1960* (New York: Atheneum, 1961), ch. 1.

70 "Kennedy chided himself . . .": O'Donnell and Powers, p. 268.

70 "Name that boy Lyndon Johnson and a heifer calf will be his": Martin, p. 230.

71 Kennedy's preparation for his inaugural address: Sorensen, *Kennedy*, p. 240.

73 Inaugural address: Sorensen, *"Let the Word Go Forth,"* pp. 12–15.

75   Meredith listens to the inaugural address: James Meredith, *Three Years in Mississippi* (Bloomington: Indiana University Press, 1966), pp. 50–54.

77   "If a Negro baby is born . . .": United States Commerce Committee, *The Joint Appearances of Senator John F. Kennedy and Vice President Richard Nixon and Other 1960 Campaign Presentations* (Washington: GPO, 1961), p. 74.

78   "Why weren't there any Negroes in that unit?": Sorensen, *Kennedy*, p. 473.

80   "Get your friends off those buses": Wofford, pp. 124–25.

82   "We don't want a lot of people getting hurt or killed down there": *Presidential Recordings Transcripts: Integration of the University of Mississippi* Dictabelt 4C, John F. Kennedy Library.

83   Meredith's arrival at Oxford: Branch, pp. 661–62.

84   "We have riots like this at Harvard just because some guy yells": *Presidential Recordings Transcripts: Integration of the University of Mississippi* Audiotape 26, John F. Kennedy Library.

86   "Let's get order up there": *Presidential Recordings Transcripts: Integration of the University of Mississippi* Dictabelt 4F, John F. Kennedy Library.

86   "It's going to be a long fall in Oxford": *Presidential Recordings Transcripts: Integration of the University of Mississippi* Audiotape 26, John F. Kennedy Library.

89   "If they shoot *you* down, they'll shoot *us* down too": Branch, pp. 837–38.

89   Civil-rights speech: Sorensen, *"Let the Word Go Forth,"* pp. 192–97.

91   The March on Washington: Sorensen, *Kennedy*, p. 504.

93   "a golden age of poetry and power": *Accent on Frost*, CBS Television, 2/1/61; Recording TNC: 190, John F. Kennedy Library.

94   "There are many kinds of courage": *Accent on Frost*.

94   JFK on the arts: *Public Papers of the Presidents of the United States, 1962* (Washington: GPO, 1963), p. 603.

94   "When power corrupts, poetry cleanses": Sorensen, *"Let the Word Go Forth,"* pp. 209–11.

95   "Prince Reindeer": Letitia Baldridge, Oral History, John F. Kennedy Library.

98   "I feel as if I've been turned into a piece of public property": Mary Barelli Gallagher, *My Life with Jacqueline Kennedy* (New York: McKay, 1969), p. 146.

99   "In eleven weeks I went from senator to president. . . .": *Public Papers of the Presidents of the United States, 1962*, p. 551.

104   JFK's affairs: Goodwin, pp. 723–25; Collier and Horowitz, pp. 174–76.

105 "Good night, pal, will you please put out the light?" O'Donnell and Powers, p. 278.

106 Céad Míle Fáilte: *Public Papers of the Presidents of the United States, 1963* (Washington: GPO, 1964), p. 540.

111 JFK's proposal for the Peace Corps: Arthur M. Schlesinger, Jr., *A Thousand Days* (Boston: Houghton Mifflin, 1965), p. 557.

113 "Only the strong, only the industrious, only the determined . . .": *Public Papers of the Presidents of the United States, 1961* (Washington: GPO, 1962), p. 205.

114 "There's a saying that victory has a hundred fathers, but defeat is an orphan": Kennedy was quoting an Italian diarist from the World War II era.

114 "The worse I do the more popular I get": Schlesinger, p. 273.

114 "I should have had Bobby in on this from the start": O'Donnell and Powers, p. 278.

114 "landing a man on the moon": Sorensen, *Let the Word Go Forth,* pp. 173–74.

115 "It will be a cold winter": Schlesinger, p. 348.

117 "I don't know enough about the Soviet Union . . .": *Presidential Recordings: The Cuban Missile Crisis,* October 16, 1962, John F. Kennedy Library.

118 Cuban Missile Crisis speech: Sorensen, *Let the Word Go Forth,* pp. 173–74.

120 Tiffany calendars: O'Donnell and Powers, p. 342.

120 Berlin speech: Sorensen, *Let the Word Go Forth,* pp. 327–28.

121 Nuclear fallout conversation: Meyers, p. 147.

123 "peace for all time": Sorensen, *Let the Word Go Forth,* pp. 282–90.

126 "Sometimes I wonder if there is something about my family that invites violence": Cameron, p. 107.

128 Children applauding: Schlesinger, p. 936.

128 Caroline asked her nanny . . . : Maud Shaw, *White House Nannie* (New York: New American Library, 1966), p. 167.

128 Two days in recent history: *Public Papers of the Presidents of the United States, 1961,* p. 786.

130 "he did not fear the weather": quoted in *Four Days: The Historical Record of the Death of President Kennedy* (New York: American Heritage, 1964), p. 138.

132 Four questions: John W. Gardner (ed.), *To Turn the Tide* (New York: Harper, 1962), pp. 35–37.

Index